Strategies for Success in Compensatory Education

STRATEGIES FOR SUCCESS IN COMPENSATORY EDUCATION:

AN APPRAISAL OF EVALUATION RESEARCH

Edward L. McDill   Mary S. McDill   J. Timothy Sprehe

The Johns Hopkins Press

Baltimore and London

To Wayland J. Hayes

CONTENTS

CONTENTS

ACKNOWLEDGMENTS

This volume is an expanded version of a paper presented at the Conference on Evaluation of Social Action Programs, May 2–3, 1969, organized by the Committee on Poverty, American Academy of Arts and Sciences, under a grant from the Ford Foundation. We are indebted to the Academy for permission to reprint the paper here in modified form.

We wish to thank James McPartland, Martha O. Roseman, and Julian C. Stanley of The Johns Hopkins University for suggestions regarding the organization and content of the document and for critical evaluation of an earlier version of the manuscript. The first author's contributions to revisions of the original paper were made possible by a Ford Foundation research fellowship.

Strategies for Success in Compensatory Education

1. FRAMEWORK FOR EVALUATION RESEARCH

Introduction

In the late 1950s and early 1960s, the social conscience of Americans was awakened to the fact that many citizens were not receiving the education which would equip them to cope in a full and useful manner with the complexities of our society. At first on the local level, and then as part of a nationwide concern for the rights and opportunities of minority groups, a massive social effort was mounted to correct this condition. Thus arose a multitude of social action programs which have been labeled "compensatory education."

In simple terms, compensatory education is education designed to compensate—to make up for some putative deficiencies in a person's learning experiences. Whether it be preschool instruction for inner-city Negroes, special efforts to lower the dropout rate among Puerto Rican teenagers, better teachers for American Indians, or vocational training for the residents of Appalachia, compensatory education has been aimed at modifying the behavior of the individual so that he can better survive in the educational system or at altering the system so that it will be more successful with students having special difficulties.

Now, a few short years after this attack on educational failure was first mustered, it is said that supplementary education itself has also failed: "Programs of compensatory education seem to have had no reliable and lasting effect. It may have been a sound political decision to launch massive compensatory programs, if only as a token of public concern. But far more was promised than we know how to deliver" (Cronbach 1969, p. 340). This contention seems borne out by the results of a carefully conducted Westinghouse study, which has recently received much publicity. The study reported that Project Head Start, one of the largest federal efforts in compensatory education, has had little impact on the learning of the thousands of preschool children it has reached (Granger et al. 1969). Whether one believes that all compensatory efforts have failed or whether

1

one argues that it is still too early to assess the extent of their impact, most observers would at least agree that the programs have <u>not</u> been demonstrated to have had widespread and dramatic success.

Several lines of reasoning have been advanced to explain this apparent failure even though there is not yet consensus that these programs have indeed failed. In a publication which has caused considerable public furor, Jensen (1969) argues that large, federally funded compensatory education efforts have been unsuccessful for reasons extrinsic to the programs themselves. They have been aimed at changing what cannot in fact be changed appreciably. Too many programs have been based on the premise that differences in intelligence are primarily a consequence of environmental variations rather than genetic factors, while compensatory education should be directed toward teaching specific academic skills (what Jensen calls "associative learning") dependent upon mental abilities more amenable to change than the I.Q.

Hunt (1969a, 1969b) differs somewhat from Jensen in his interpretation of the evidence. For example, Jensen contends that almost every child has an adequate physical and social environment for learning and that sensory deprivation is not a factor in cognitive development beyond a certain critical, low-level threshold. However, Hunt notes that a wide range of sensory deprivations can cause chemical reactions in the body. Biological changes in the young child stem from these reactions and cannot be isolated from his genetic endowment at birth. Hunt's contention is that the environment does affect a child's behavior and that its impact begins to be felt when he is still an infant in the crib. Thus he would argue that compensatory education should be begun when the child is a few days or a few months old. The child should be subjected to an enriched environment offering a variety of stimuli and providing reinforcement for those which are conducive to mental development. Hunt counts himself "among the few who are inclined to believe that mankind has not yet developed and deployed a form of early childhood education (from birth to age five) which permits him to achieve his full genotypic potential" (1969b, p. 292). In this view, the failure of compensatory education is the result of

2

the delay in introducing it into the life of the disadvantaged child.

There is a third viewpoint, represented by Elkind (1969) and elaborated by him in response to the Jensen paper. We disagree with much—in fact, with almost all—of Elkind's arguments,[1] and summarize them here with the proviso that we consider them speculative and without a sound theoretical base, although his conclusion may have some merit independent of the manner in which it is presented. Preschool instruction has failed, says Elkind, because the intellectual development of children cannot be accelerated by compensatory schooling; what is being taught at this young age should be left for elementary school. He agrees that there are crucial periods in a child's development but argues that these occur not at preschool but rather at elementary school age. He cites Piaget's observation that a certain stage of intellectual development is attained by all children at about the same time, six or seven years of age, regardless of their cultural or socioeconomic experience: "Apparently, therefore, environmental variation during the

---

[1]We cannot discuss these disagreements here in detail. However, we will briefly state some of them.

(a) Elkind uses in his argument for elementary level programs the Piagetian theory that the same stage of development is reached by all children, regardless of cultural and socioeconomic background, at approximately six years of age. However, he insists upon the interdependence of each stage of development with the preceding stage, i.e., one stage acts as an organizer for the next higher stage (pp. 325–26). These two observations seem incompatible with the notion that failure occurs at the elementary school level. One could argue with equal logic that if the "expected" stage of development has not been reached by disadvantaged children, then a deficit could have occurred at the stage which acts as the organizing stage for the elementary school level of development, namely, the preschool level. (The scant evidence we have—Title I projects at the elementary level—has certainly not shown success.)

(b) As evidence for his statement that preschool instruction has not been demonstrated to have <u>lasting</u> effects on mental

elementary school period is more significant for later intellectual attainments of the Piagetian variety. In short, there is not much justification for making the preschool the scapegoat for our failures in elementary education. Like it or not, the years from six to twelve are the crucial ones with respect to later academic achievement" (p. 333). Elkind concludes that a more profitable application of effort would be a restructuring of the elementary school so that at this period of his development the child would have uninterrupted blocks of time in which his own intrinsic motivation for learning could surface.

In the face of the current controversies surrounding compensatory education, we are disposed to ask: what does the available evidence show? Conclusions about the success or failure of compensatory education are only as meaningful as the empirical evidence upon which they are based. Are the evaluations which have been conducted methodologically sound? Can they be used as evidence of the success or failure of efforts at compensatory education, or are further studies necessary before we can argue from a theory about the causes of failure in current endeavors and then proceed to explore the new directions and modifications in an attempt to educate disadvantaged children successfully?

---

growth, Elkind refers (p. 331) to two studies conducted in the 1940s. These studies were based upon traditional, play-oriented, middle-class nursery schools. He does not consider the intensive, cognitive-oriented preschool instruction (discussed below) which has recently been used with disadvantaged preschoolers and which does seem to have a positive effect. Granted, these programs have not been in existence long enough to provide definitive evidence to accept or refute Elkind's argument; that is, longitudinal, cognitive data are not available on adults exposed to these programs which can be compared with that for adults not enrolled in them (see Chapter 4 below for further discussion of this position). However, Karnes (1968), using the Bereiter-Engelmann (1966) approach, reports that cognitive gains achieved during the first year of exposure not only did not fade out during the second year but actually increased.

4

Almost all programs contain—often are required by law to contain—provisions for evaluation of their impact. Agencies responsible for carrying out compensatory education have had to conduct more or less scientific studies to determine whether or not they have effected the desired changes. These voluminous research findings are the "data" to which we have directed our attention. They cover small projects involving only fifteen pre-school students; they cover vast federal programs reaching hundreds of cities and millions of students, with budgets in the billions. As might be expected, the quality of the research is, to say the least, uneven, ranging from carefully conceived experimental designs to solicited testimonials.

In sifting through these materials, we have addressed ourselves to three important problems concerning compensatory educational programs. First, there is the problem of the quality of evaluation research on these programs to date. How good is it from a scientific standpoint? Second, we have sought knowledge as to the effectiveness of compensatory education, based on such evaluations. Where research is of acceptable quality, what does it tell us about the success of the program? Third, we have examined the implications of the data both for the future planning of compensatory education programs and for designing studies to test their effectiveness. What lessons can be learned concerning successful compensatory education and its measurement?

Our investigation has been deliberately limited to compensatory education in academic settings. Thus we exclude community action and manpower programs, which are primarily designed to upgrade occupational skills or provide other employment-related assistance to needy persons but which might also use remedial education as part of such assistance. These limitations seem necessary in order to arrive at generalizations from such a vast body of literature.

Overview of Problems in Action Research

Evaluation research on any and all compensatory programs is supposedly used as a basis for decision-making regarding either the survival of a given program or its future direction. Accordingly, it is an instrument of policy-making, subject to political factors beyond its control, such as funding levels being determined by outside authorities and the press for regional balance in the allocation of funds. Not surprisingly, the tone and style of some evaluation research resemble the hortatory political tract. On the other hand, evaluation research does serve to advance scientific knowledge about the individual and society, and for this reason it should be conducted by disinterested and unbiased persons. However, the administration of the program to be evaluated—particularly in the case of new, untried programs—is best handled by interested and favorably biased people.

Both the policy-maker and the research scientist want the program to "work," but often for different reasons: the one wants efficient and uninterrupted administration of one particular program and the other wants positive findings subject to scientific generalization. The scientist seeks a rigorous research design which will make for ready generalization of his findings; the administrator often seeks only concrete answers to his own specific questions. This disparity has important conditioning effects on the scientific as well as the practical outcomes of the research, for one quickly finds that the scientific evaluation of a compensatory education program is intimately bound up with its administrative design—the provision for evaluation within the design, the nature of program objectives, and the specific means for achieving those objectives. Not infrequently, the goals of evaluation research and the objectives of the program come into conflict. We shall cite some specific instances of this conflict below.

One may venture the suggestion that those having a strong academic bias will probably lean toward the belief that weaknesses in compensatory education programs stem almost wholly from the involvement in them of politicians and bureaucrats. In some important respects this seems not to be the case, and attention should be turned toward difficulties which are properly the responsibility of the research scientist.

The Nature of the Development Process
and Attendant Problems

There are a number of general problems in compensatory education which are encountered because of the nature of educational variables, regardless of whether these variables make their appearance in research on a compensatory program or in the conventional school setting.

(a) Program Effects or Maturational Effects? Most compensatory education programs are aimed at the preschool and elementary school child. Both governmental administrators (Nixon 1969) and the academic community (Bloom 1964, Deutsch 1967) have agreed that it is best to "get 'em while they're young." Much of this emphasis is probably attributable to the current philosophy of poverty in the United States, that is, the belief in "cumulative deficits" operating over the life cycle such that by the time a youth reaches adolescence he is already so disadvantaged that only prohibitively expensive and time-consuming compensatory programs can have much effect.[2]

In research at the preschool level it is extremely difficult to know whether programs are found to be ineffective (a) because they really are deficient or (b) because research scientists are simply not able to assess the impact of the program because the critical variables are unknown or cannot be measured adequately.

Compensatory education or no compensatory education, we simply do not know much about how preschool children learn, and we know even less about disadvantaged learners. We do not know what proportion of the measured differences in pre- and post-test scores on standardized tests are attributable to the program and how much to "natural" variations in rates of maturation in the cognitive domain for any given cohort.[3]

---

[2]Rapidly changing political conditions in this country may well result in more emphasis being placed on adolescents.

[3]As Campbell (1957, p. 298) notes, maturation has been a chronic problem in research in child development, experimental social psychology, and education, and in such research

Piaget (1952, 1963), for example, conceives the development of intellectual functioning as a progression through stages which are both qualitatively different and discontinuous with respect to one another. As he enters each stage, the child goes through a process of reorganizing his cognitive structures. This reorganization is seen as a consequence of his adaptation to his environment. If Piaget's theory is taken as valid, then it becomes important to ascertain the optimum time to intervene with a compensatory education program and to know where the program is impinging on the child relative to his stage-by-stage development. One must also take into consideration the further complication that there might be differences in the rates of movement from one intellectual stage to the next which are associated with subcultural differences based on social class, race, and ethnic background. The same program could conceivably have quite different effects, depending on its relationship to developmental stages among various subcultural groups.

Bruner (1966) suggests that intellectual development involves a process whereby a stimulus is controlled in such a

---

one or more control groups must be set up to determine its effect. However, as noted below, evaluation studies frequently do not employ randomly assigned experimental and control groups. Furthermore, even the most carefully designed experiments in laboratory settings have inherent weaknesses which seriously limit the degree to which they can be generalized to the solution of practical problems in natural settings. However, only part of this problem is mitigated by the use of control groups. Even more important is the impossibility of controlling extraneous factors impinging on the experiment. This problem becomes increasingly crucial as the time interval in a program of "treatment" increases. If, for example, we do not know how peer relationships affect instructional rates and if they are not randomly distributed, the program could be seriously biased. We know, for instance, that peer relationships vary with sex, but we do not know how they affect cognitive development. There may be other such variables which have not been examined. The discussion of socializing agents will examine this problem further.

way that the response to it is not directly predictable. At present, we know little about the mechanisms by which children, whether middle-class or socially disadvantaged, transform their responses so that these responses become increasingly independent. Evaluation research necessarily suffers from the lack of systematic scientific knowledge concerning such intellectual processes, upon which compensatory education is designed to have an impact.

The confounding of maturational and program effects is also related to the structure of research design. The scientist usually employs the conventional "black box" strategy (Hawkridge, Chalupsky, and Roberts 1968, Pt. 1, p. 17) because he lacks the knowledge to do otherwise. He chooses one point of input and one of output in a complex process of child development and restricts his observations to these two points. What he does not know, in our present state of knowledge, is whether the points chosen represent—in fact, or even in theory—some real points of input and output in the life cycle of the child. In fact, he frequently does not concern himself with the correspondence between maturational stages and his chosen input/output points. As one recent critic has put it, "The problem, then, is reduced to finding the appropriate inputs for achieving the desired output. While schematically this may appear to be an accurate analysis of the problem, it bypasses the critical intervening and mediating factor—the child. Nowhere does one find a description of the four-year-old child, a developmental analysis of the personality and cognitive functioning of children at this age level, or a statement of their primary areas of conflict, typical modes of resolution, and principal spheres of development" (Zimiles 1969, p. 179). The points of input/output measurement are just as likely to be incorrect as correct: the research design may be looking at the wrong things in relation to the maturation of the child.

This line of thought can be summarized in more conventional terms by saying that social scientists have poorly substantiated ideas as to whether there are such things as "delayed effects" and "undetected changes," and whether long-term rather than short-term evaluation of compensatory education programs is needed. And let it be stressed again that what is

9

in question here is social science theory, not a strategy of planned intervention. At present, controversies about delayed effects or undetected changes are unresolvable and therefore are particularly vulnerable to ideology and partisan reasoning. There may be delayed effects and there may not be; we do not yet know. Similarly, compensatory education may be highly effective and it may not be; we do not know.

(b) Interaction of Various Socializing Agencies. A second general difficulty is that education does not take place exclusively in schools. The family and other out-of-school environments constitute important settings for learning—learning that may or may not be compatible with that in the program. There are interactions between the child's experiences in school and those in the family and neighborhood and peer group. Evaluators are faced with the difficulty of assessing both the explicit and implicit effects of these confounding influences. Trying to control scientifically only what occurs within a compensatory education program may approach futility, for the scientist may be dealing with intervention which has only a weak effect upon the child.[4] Nor do we know the dynamics of interaction between home and school. Are there circumstances in which the family cancels out the effects of the school, and others in which it compounds the school's effect? McDill, Rigsby, and Meyers (1969), in a large-scale study of schools, present evidence which strongly suggests that a chief source of variation in the "climate" effects of high schools on the achievement of students is the extent of parental and community involvement in the school.

The difficulty could be favorably resolved by directing attention to interaction effects between school and home settings and then designing programs such that the school would be a sociopsychological agent complementary to that of the home. Bloom (1966) argues that, when school and home are mutually

_____

[4] For example, Coleman et al. (1966) found that the variation in achievement within schools was approximately four times as large as the variation between schools. In addition, a large part of the variation in individual achievement was accounted for by characteristics of family background.

reinforcing, the optimal conditions are present for the child's cognitive development. Unless the home effect is identified as either adversative or complementary to the school, however, a given compensatory education program is doomed to conflict with more powerful socializing agencies.

(c) Technology. Even when one has a firm idea of the variables which are important in a program design, that is, when the investigator knows exactly what the criterion and predictor variables are, there is still the question of measurement. Intelligence tests, developed over decades of systematic and intensive research, are among the more adequate measures of human abilities. These tests represent the developed technology, the "hardware," as it were, of the educational psychologist. Such a technology is largely lacking for the crucial tasks facing evaluation research, and the "state of the art" of evaluation suffers from the underdevelopment in technology.

The importance of this underdevelopment is that compensatory education is heavily aimed at the preschool population. At this level, the more widely known ability and achievement tests for children have limitations which are so acute that some observers (Bereiter 1967, p. 358) have questioned the validity of changes in scores on such instruments. It has been necessary to construct new instruments to assess how well a given preschool curriculum has met its instructional objectives. Bereiter (1967, p. 358) gives as an example the Concept Inventory test, developed by his colleague, Engelmann, which he feels is the only test available for adequately measuring the language skills toward which his program is directed.

If it is true that the state of development of cognitive skill tests at the preschool level is rather primitive, the picture is even bleaker when one moves to the affective domain. The development of tests at the preschool level is only a more dramatic illustration of what is found at all other age levels, namely, that there have been more strides forward in test measurement in the cognitive domain than in the socioemotional or attitudinal domain, yet the vast majority of compensatory education programs have "personality" development as their target variable. Sometimes such development is as heavily emphasized as is acquisition of cognitive skills.

Personality variables, as distinguished from strictly cognitive ones, are known to be important for compensatory education. For example, the Coleman report (Coleman et al. 1966) finds that a "control of environment" is the single variable most highly correlated with the academic achievement of disadvantaged students. Clearly this is a variable in the affective domain—an aspect of the child's self-concept. Yet we have no tests which measure self-concept with anything like the rigor and frequent replication of intelligence tests. There are no such tests which have been normed on the entire population. The intelligence quotient is a statistic very important in our educational system as well as in the larger society and there is a similar need of a self-concept quotient. There is no such statistic at present. Still, the child's personality, in educational programs, is consistently dichotomized[5] into a cognitive and an affective domain. Both, however, continue to be assessed in terms of intelligence tests designed only to measure the former.

To take another example, many researchers concerned with teacher effectiveness have pointed to the importance of teacher "warmth" for student motivation and achievement. Certain behavioral characteristics of teachers are thought to have positive effects on the student's self-concept, which in turn has a positive effect on learning. Yet systematic empirical evidence on this affective aspect of teacher effectiveness is lacking. One can assume with some justification that one of the important reasons for this is the absence of a hard technology to assess the impact of variables such as "warmth."

In sum, although compensatory education programs continue to be focused on the affective or socioemotional development of the child, in assessing them one is still required to accept subjective evaluations because rigorous measuring instruments are lacking.

---

[5]Psychologists frequently use the "trichotomy" of cognitive, affective, and psychomotor domains.

We have in this section directed attention to the larger framework within which compensatory education programs operate. We would like once again to emphasize that these problems are not evaluation design problems, but even so, they are intimately linked with evaluation and its outcomes.

2. DESCRIPTION AND ANALYSIS OF COMPREHENSIVE PROGRAMS

We will present descriptive and evaluative information on two different responses to the need for compensatory education for disadvantaged groups. In the first category are agencies having comprehensive, multipurpose objectives which are federally financed and were created as a part of the war on poverty legislation during the Johnson Administration. These agencies do not implement action programs to achieve their goals; they are primarily administrative units whose most important function is policy determination and who use outside agencies to implement these goals. There are three such administrative units spanning the preschool, elementary, and secondary range of special education which will be considered below, Head Start, Title I, and Upward Bound. After the discussion of these three programs, we will consider the second category, local programs, and give examples of the types of programs which have been initiated.

Head Start

Head Start was designed as an intervention program for disadvantaged preschool children to prepare them to cope with later school life successfully and to prevent developmental deficits which would hamper their success. In order to achieve this broad objective, the program adopted a multifaceted approach, involving efforts to improve intellectual and academic performance and physical health, and to provide social services and psychological services as well as to involve parents in the program itself (McDavid et al. n.d.).

Head Start began as an eight-week pilot program in the summer of 1965, under the aegis of the Office of Economic Opportunity (OEO), with an enrollment of slightly more than 500,000 children. At the end of that summer it was announced that the program would be expanded to include full-year services. Currently (1969), 450,000 children are enrolled in the summer and 214,000 in the full-year program.

In fiscal year 1970 approximately half the summer programs will be converted to full-year programs. Enrollments are then expected to be 225,000 for the summer and 260,000 for the full year. Head Start has a total estimated budget of $330 million for fiscal year 1969. However, only $6 million (less than 2 percent) of this amount is allocated for research and evaluation. The program is carried on in local centers, totaling more than 13,000 as of 1967. Their emphasis appears to have varied tremendously both in terms of academic curriculum and auxiliary services provided, thus rendering systematic evaluation a difficult task. However, OEO has maintained its own research and evaluation unit from the inception of the program and has made attempts, subject to restrictions imposed by financial and personnel limitations, to appraise the work of the multitude of local centers with different objectives and to generate ideas for innovation in the program.

The volume of available research studies and those planned in the future for Head Start far exceeds that of either the Upward Bound or Title I programs. There are several possible reasons for this. First, the program has been in existence since 1965, longer than the other two. Second, a more innovative approach has been taken to it because it has represented a national effort to extend formal or systematic education "downward," providing preschool education where none existed before for most children and certainly not for the vast majority of disadvantaged children. It was also innovative in that heretofore there had been little interest in training the preschool child to acquire cognitive or school skills. Of course, this was partly because of the middle-class orientation toward socioemotional development which pervaded preschool institutions. Third, national interest and enthusiasm were expressed for Head Start right from the beginning, with attendant expectations beyond the capabilities of any program and certainly beyond those of any newly structured program. Recently, both the public in general and the government in particular have demanded to know to what extent these expectations have been realized. Such an evaluation has become increasingly necessary as federal funding for educational programs has been cut back and, of course, as Head Start's critics continue to insist that the whole program should be abolished and new approaches sought.

One of our more amazing discoveries in preparing this study was how evaluations of Head Start have proliferated during the short time that our analysis has been in progress, an indication of the awareness of the need for such information. In an attempt to obtain some degree of closure on the extent of evaluation in the massive Head Start effort, we have relied heavily on a number of summaries ranging from in-house documents prepared by the research and evaluation unit of Head Start to the first issue of a bulletin devoted to communicating information on research activities to the education community (Headstart Childhood Research Information Bulletin, 1969).

A fairly recent summary of research and evaluation studies prepared by the evaluation and research unit (Research and Evaluation, Project Headstart, January, 1968) reveals their variety and magnitude, arranged according to subject matter:

Subject Matter	Completed Studies	Ongoing Studies
Curriculum	6[a]	12
Teachers	7	5
Learning	—	20
Parents	16[b]	26
Follow-up	13	8
Language and cognitive behavior	9	23
Measuring instruments	8	16
Health and physical development	—	2
Motivation	1	1
Special problems[c]	—	1

[a]Excludes two demonstration projects.

[b]Excludes one demonstration project.

[c]Programs for emotionally disturbed children.

These studies include both national assessments and circumscribed individual evaluation efforts. The large bulk of the completed studies are descriptive, and the quality of the majority is well below the standards which one would wish to be applied in formulating changes or choosing among alternatives. We make this statement with the full realization that most of the studies were undertaken shortly after the program began and, no doubt, was suffering from many administrative problems.

It is interesting to note the contrast between the completed evaluation studies and the ongoing projects. Ongoing studies seem to be moving in new directions: for example, measuring instruments are receiving more attention, as are language and cognitive behavior. In the earlier studies dealing with parents, many of the projects merely attempted to describe and characterize the family atmosphere, home conditions, and family stability from which Head Start children come. However, ongoing studies seem to be concentrated more on the role which parents play in the child's acquisition of skills, as manifested, for example, in the interaction between mother and child.

In studies dealing with curriculum, the usual attempt was to compare the different curricula, such as Montessori, traditional, or structured. The results were as follows:

	No Effect	Mixed	Positive Effect
Montessori	1		2
Traditional	1		
Structured		1	1

There is very little evidence here upon which one could conclude with much confidence that one type of program curriculum is more highly effective than any other in achieving cognitive gains. There is one very noteworthy local study not included in the document used for this review to which attention should be called. It is Rusk's study (1969) comparing a structured and a traditional Head Start program. We shall not include a review of his results here, as they are more appropriately

17

discussed below. However, he presents a review and summary of several evaluations of a comparative nature. His conclusion, based on both his own research and evidence from other studies, is that the most highly effective curricula are those of a structured nature. This finding is, of course, not incompatible with those cited above.

Follow-up has been one of the areas which has received most attention, partially in response to charges that the initial gains made in the Head Start program are lost over time (frequently referred to as the "fadeout" or "leveling-off" effect). There has been an increase in the sophistication of the research in this area. The later studies have profited from the mistakes made by the earlier ones and pointed out by critics, such as their lack of pretests and control groups.

Another useful document in attempting to assess the evaluation of Head Start's effects on cognitive growth to date is the first issue of a bulletin prepared by the ERIC Center of the National Laboratory on Early Childhood Education (Headstart Childhood Research Information Bulletin, 1969). The issue contains abstracts of fifty-five relevant, completed studies of Head Start activities in the years 1965 through 1967. We uncovered eleven additional relevant research projects not covered in the Bulletin. An analysis of these sixty-six evaluations reveals some interesting statistics on the impact of the program during this period, if one makes the assumption that these studies are representative of evaluation efforts during the first three years. They range from modest local efforts to assessments at the national level. (A number of these studies are included in the table on p. 16.) Thirty-five of these assessments are excluded from this discussion because they present no evidence, pro or con, on cognitive growth.[1]

---

[1]We readily acknowledge that restricting our consideration to evidence of cognitive growth does not permit any conclusions about the impact of the program in other crucial areas such as families and the neighborhoods or communities in which Head Start centers are located. However, even though the instruments for measuring cognitive growth in preschool

Seventeen of the thirty-one studies which present some evidence on cognitive variables are reported as having used control groups in a before-after design; fourteen used before-after comparisons without control groups. However, even in the seventeen studies employing control groups, random assignment of students to one or the other category was the exception, thus necessitating caution in drawing conclusions about purported effects. More important, however, is the fact that only eleven of the thirty-one studies appear to have shown clearly positive effects of Head Start experiences on cognitive development.

A series of documents prepared by the Department of Health, Education, and Welfare to brief the recently formed Advisory Committee on Head Start at its meeting of March 7–8, 1969, provides some useful information on the results of evaluation efforts to date and on large-scale evaluations currently under way. One of these documents (Headstart Report, p. 1) states: "There is mounting evidence that Headstart has not yet proved as effective as had earlier been thought. Preliminary reports from a major evaluation soon to be completed suggest that, so far, its long-term effects have been slight."

This conclusion corresponds to ours, based on a number of evaluation studies and summaries of evaluation efforts. We also conclude that the available evidence of a positive nature is based on research which often has such serious methodological weaknesses (especially a failure to obtain pre- and post-measures) that unequivocal conclusions are difficult to draw. However, major national-level assessments are described (Headstart Report, Attachment C) which appear to be more rigorous than earlier national-level attempts and, therefore, should soon provide more valid evidence on the impact of Head Start.

---

children are crude, they are much more adequate than those for assessing the program's impact on families or communities, which often take the form of "testimonials" or the investigator's subjective impressions. Furthermore, in this study our primary concern is, of necessity, with the degree of impact of compensatory education on cognitive functioning.

The national study, which, in our view, is the most comprehensive and systematic to date, has just been completed. Because its findings and conclusions have produced so much controversy among both researchers and politicians, it will be discussed in some detail. The research, published as The Impact of Head Start (Granger et al. 1969), hereafter referred to as the Westinghouse study, was conducted by the Westinghouse Learning Corporation and Ohio University under contract with OEO during 1968–1969. It was focused on a highly critical question: to what extent has the Head Start program as a whole had an impact on the psychological and intellectual development of children which has persisted into the elementary school years? Two of the most refreshing aspects of the study are the authors' acute awareness of its limitations, both in focus and methodology. Both of these shortcomings are primarily attributable to circumstances beyond the control of the researchers. Nevertheless, this has not deterred a number of social scientists, congressmen, federal executives, and journalists from criticizing the validity of the results and the authors' conclusion that "the Head Start children cannot be said to be appreciably different from their peers in the elementary grades who did not attend Head Start in most aspects of cognitive and affective development measured in this study with the exception of the slight but nonetheless significant superiority of full-year Head Start children on certain measures of cognitive development" (p. 8). We will return to these criticisms below.

The researchers used a sample of 1,980 first-, second-, and third-grade students from 104 Head Start centers and a matched sample of nonparticipating children from the same schools as controls in conducting the evaluation. The two groups were matched on the key variables of age, sex, race/ethnicity, and kindergarten attendance. The socioeconomic status of the two groups was rendered comparable by use of covariance techniques when the data were analyzed. A battery of mental aptitude, scholastic achievement, and attitudinal tests was administered to both groups. In addition, interview data were obtained from the students, their parents, and officials of the Head Start centers. Finally, teachers of both groups of students completed rating forms on such aspects of their pupils' behavior as desire for achievement and motivation for learning; they also assessed the intellectual and social climate of their schools.

The primary analyses of these data were conducted using covariance techniques for both Head Start centers and individual students as units. The results were checked against those obtained from a nonparametric technique. The authors report that generally similar results were obtained by these different approaches to the data. The following are some of the more important findings from the separate analyses of summer and full-year programs and of grade level of students for the total national sample:

(a) On a measure of language development, the Illinois Test of Psycholinguistic Abilities, no statistically significant differences were found between the Head Start subjects and their counterparts at any of the three grade levels for the summer programs. For full-year programs, on two of the subtests Head Start pupils were favored.

(b) On the Metropolitan Readiness Tests, a measure of learning readiness to enter school, Head Start children in the first grade who had been enrolled in full-year programs achieved significantly (but only slightly) higher than controls on two subscores, but no differences were obtained between Head Start summer participants and the controls.

(c) No significant differences were found between first- and second-grade Head Start and control groups on the Stanford Achievement Tests (a general measure of academic achievement). This finding also held for both summer school and full-year second-grade participants. Likewise, there were no differences between summer school participants and controls at grade three. The number of full-year Head Start centers for children who were in grade three when the evaluation was conducted was too small to permit an adequate assessment of the program's effects at this grade level.

(d) The Head Start participants from both full-year and summer programs did not score significantly higher than the controls at any of the three grade levels on a number of measures of affective variables: self-concept, desire for achievement, and attitudes toward significant others such as parents, peers, and society at large.

Thus for the national sample (that is, for the program as a whole) only four small, statistically significant differences were found when a large number of comparisons were made on a battery containing six different mental tests.

Given the limitations of their post hoc design (that is, the possible sources of uncontrolled variation), the Westinghouse researchers were forced to admit the possibility that, at the national level, the Head Start experience had produced short-run effects which did not persist for one or more reasons.

Some of the explanations which they offered for their results are as follows:

(a) Head Start does have an impact on children, but its facilitative effects are counteracted or nullified by the adverse environment of the typically nonstimulating school in which these children receive their elementary level education. However, a separate analysis conducted by the Westinghouse researchers (pp. 190−95) does not support this "immediacy effect" argument. It was tested by dividing the students into two groups, those who went directly from Head Start into first grade and those who went to kindergarten. The reasoning was that if the immediacy phenomenon were operating, differences in the cognitive and affective measures between Head Start and controls (for each group) should be greater for those going directly to first grade than for those who had the additional experience of a year in kindergarten. The analysis was conducted separately for summer and full-year Head Start programs and by grade in school (first, second, or third). No over-all, consistent results were found which would permit a clear acceptance or rejection of the proposition. More important, however, the variable "immediate effect of Head Start experience" explained almost none of the variance in children's scores on any of the criterion measures.

(b) A period of rapid development occurs in the early elementary years for those children not attending Head Start programs; that is, Head Start does have a significant effect, but those not exposed to it have a cognitive "spurt" as a consequence of their regular school experience which results in their catching up with Head Start children. This interpretation is consistent with the observations of child psychologists and educational measurement specialists that shortly after they first enter the school situation, children tend to experience a period of rapid intellectual development.

(c) The presence of Head Start children in classrooms with nonparticipants produces a contagion effect which raises the level of performance and aspirations of those not exposed to the program.

(d) Where local programs have been properly designed and executed, they produce significant benefits. Implicit in this speculation is the belief that at the national level the effectiveness of the well-run centers is counteracted by the ineffectiveness of those with poorly implemented programs.

Clearly, none of these speculations is inconsistent with the Westinghouse conclusion that Head Start, to date, has not produced widespread significant gains of a cognitive and socioemotional nature which are maintained in the primary grades. Only protracted, intensive, longitudinal research which includes data on variations in programs across Head Start centers and which follows students through the primary grades can shed light on the validity of the four lines of argument posed above. However, to us none of these explanations has much appeal, given the fact that the negative results of the Westinghouse study are consistent with the few earlier longitudinal studies employing experimental designs. Rather, we are inclined to take the position that over-all, systematic changes have not been produced by Head Start, as it is presently constituted.

As noted earlier, the Westinghouse study has been stingingly criticized from a variety of quarters. Because we believe some of the criticisms to be invalid and others to be based on aspects of the study totally beyond the control of the evaluators, we feel it important to discuss them at some length and to attempt to rebut those which are unreasonable.

One of the most frequently cited criticisms is that the study is too limited in scope, focusing only on cognitive and affective criterion measures (New York Times 1969b, p. 22). We may grant that it did not attempt to assess the impact of Head Start on the physical health, nutrition, social services, family stability, or larger community of the child, each of which is an important objective of the program. However, in our view, the researchers were completely justified in re-stricting their focus to two types of psychological variables, as the time and funds available were inadequate to assess all objectives of the program. Furthermore, it seems safe to say that most people who value social action programs would agree that the two criteria selected for study are among the most im-portant objectives of such programs. This was certainly true of the original OEO planning committee for Head Start, com-posed of scientists and academicians, who were charged by the federal government with establishing objectives and guidelines. The panel focused its attention on the development of a program which would be effective in increasing achievement and oppor-tunities for socially disadvantaged children (Improving the Opportunities and Achievements of the Children of the Poor, February, 1965). Finally, when the Westinghouse researchers state that choosing these two categories of variables involves posing questions which are the "right ones to ask first" (p. 2), their implicit position is difficult to refute: namely, that one of the prime objectives in improving the nutrition, physical health, and social services of children is to enhance their cog-nitive development.

A second criticism leveled at the Westinghouse study is that the measures of the criterion variables, especially those dealing with affective criteria, are of "dubious validity" (New Republic 1969). We have lamented the lack of adequate meas-ures of cognitive and affective development of young children (see pp. 11–12 above). Certainly the Westinghouse team was aware of this problem, for they found it necessary to devise their own instruments in an attempt to provide measures of self-concept, achievement motivation, and attitudes toward significant others in the environment. Although these measures have many imperfections, the coefficients of reliability (both internal consistency and test-retest coefficients) and validity obtained are above the minimum levels of acceptability generally established by educational measurement specialists. In short, although these measures are admitted by the research team to be somewhat crude, they are far more valid scientifically than the subjective impressions and testimonials often proferred by other researchers in the field.

With respect to the cognitive tests employed in the research, a much stronger defense can be made, although highly precise measures of mental aptitude and achievement for young children are yet to be developed. All three tests employed—the Metropolitan Readiness Tests, the Stanford Achievement Tests, and the Illinois Test of Psycholinguistic Abilities—have been in use for several years and have been normed on national samples of students. Furthermore, all three tests have been employed extensively in numerous studies of students in the Head Start age ranges and have shown an over-all high level of reliability and validity.

Another criticism of the evaluation, which is not without some justification, is the ex post facto design of the evaluation, which we have noted earlier. However, this is a shortcoming which was beyond the control of the researchers, who were charged by OEO with the responsibility of providing, in a short period of time, objective evidence on the consequences of the program. To date OEO has been unable to mount a continuing, systematic, nationwide program of evaluation of Head Start, and the researchers had no opportunity to conduct a longitudinal assessment which could provide more definitive answers to critical questions about the program's effectiveness. In the absence of such an opportunity, they matched subjects on a number of important background variables and introduced one of the most powerful statistical tools available, analysis of covariance, to control another important background factor, socioeconomic status of the child's family, and also to determine the effects of the Head Start experience. In short, given the problems inherent in the research questions, their research design and analysis are not only defensible but commendable.

25

There is another criticism to which we shall briefly address ourselves: the researchers ignored the fact that Head Start is a heterogeneous collection of local centers which vary greatly in the nature and quality of their efforts. To lump the local centers together for purposes of analysis and to treat them as a homogeneous program masks important differences in centers and possibly a varied impact on students (New York Times 1969a, p. 11E). Clearly, this is a limitation of the study and involves an important research question which must be answered as quickly as possible. However, the failure of the Westinghouse team to answer this question in no sense vitiates the importance of the global and more fundamental question of the effects of the program to date on the national level. When asked recently what the "independent variable" was in the Head Start program (and thus, by implication, in the Westinghouse evaluation), one former OEO official responded, "$300 million for FY 69." To this we would merely add that Head Start is a nationwide program and therefore that it is not only proper but essential that evaluations of its impact be conducted at the national level.

There are other criticisms, of varying degrees of validity, which have been leveled at the study concerning such matters as the inadequacy of the sample in terms of size and representativeness and its failure to consider either the likely effects of variation in the quality of schools attended since Head Start upon the criterion variables or the effects of Head Start children upon other children in the classroom. As mentioned earlier, the last two considerations were offered by the Westinghouse researchers as possible explanations for their empirical results, and they made some attempt to gather evidence on this issue, reflecting a high degree of research sophistication on their part.

The question of sample adequacy is a highly complex one in any national study, especially one involving different levels of units of analysis. There are certain characteristics of the sampling design which make the sample vulnerable to criticism. However, there is no reason to believe that it is not sufficiently representative to permit valid generalizations about the impact of Head Start. For example, in a comparison of nonparticipating and participating centers, statistically significant differences were found in only five characteristics out of thirty-two. A comparison of the sample centers with a larger sample of centers selected by the Bureau of the Census showed no startling differences in terms of characteristics such as sex ratio of pupils, father's education, and racial/ethnic distribution of pupils.

To summarize, although the Westinghouse study has all the defects inherent in nonexperimental research, it is by far the most rigorous national assessment of Head Start which has been undertaken since the program's inception. In closing this discussion, we would like to pose a question: would this study have been subjected to such strong criticism from so many quarters had it shown an over-all positive effect rather than essentially no effect? It is our opinion that some social researchers, educators, and program administrators have become so involved personally in social action programs that they are unable to accept the apparent failure of many of them as a challenge and to modify them in the hope of obtaining better results in the future. Instead, many such people have a tendency to take a defensive stance and to express the fear that the federal government is going to "shut up shop": "To be truly scientific we must be able to experiment. We must be able to advocate without that excess of commitment that blinds us to reality testing" (Campbell 1969, p. 410).

Title I

Title I of the Elementary and Secondary Education Act, launched in 1966 under the administrative cognizance of the U.S. Office of Education (USOE), has as its ultimate goal the overcoming of educational deprivation associated with poverty and race. More specifically, its objectives are not only to decrease achievement differences correlated with race and social class but to provide medical and dental services, lunch programs, teacher training, diagnostic services, and classroom construction. The allocation of Title I funds involves block aid to the states based on applications submitted to each state by its educational agencies.

Title I has as its target populations students at the pre-school, elementary, and secondary levels, including dropouts. However, it has thus far concentrated on the early elementary years. At the preschool level it has made possible the development of special curricula focusing on cognitive skills—especially reading, arithmetic, and language. Its other efforts include an extended school day or year to help counteract the typical "cumulative deficits" accruing over the conventional nine-month school year. Funds are used for classroom aides, often parents of disadvantaged children, whose responsibilities range from child-tending to clerical and tutorial work with individual students. Funds are also used for the recruitment and training of teachers whose specialty is teaching socially disadvantaged children.

Since the inception of the program, 13,000 school districts have received Title I funds. Appropriations were $979 million for 1965–1966, $1.053 billion for 1966–1967, and $1.191 billion for 1967–1968; the appropriation for FY 1969 is $1.123 billion. To give some idea of the enormous number of children affected, in preschool alone 475,000 students participated in Title I programs during 1966–1967. In terms of dollar investments and number of students participating, Title I is the largest compensatory education program in existence.

There was a small amount of research, primarily descriptive in nature, conducted during 1965–1966, the first year of the program, but it will not be reviewed here.[2] The most comprehensive evaluation of the effects of Title I on academic achievement of participating students in its second year was commissioned by USOE (Title I/Year II n.d., pp. 24–35). Data were requested from the one hundred largest central city school systems in the United States; eighty responded in some way. However, a substantial number of the responses had to be discarded because of various inadequacies, and only thirty-nine cities were included

---

[2]The interested reader may consult U.S., Department of Health, Education, and Welfare, The First Year of Title I, ESEA: The States Report (Washington, D.C.: U.S. Government Printing Office, 1966).

in the analysis, which focused on standardized reading test scores. Since the scores reported were for a variety of reading tests, the analyst was forced to use percentile or grade equivalent scores in his analysis. In addition, adjustments had to be made to try to obtain a common pretest–post-test interval.

Grade equivalent data covered 38,500 students in twenty-two of the thirty-nine "usable" cities; data which ranked students by quarter of national norm groups were available for 29,000 pupils in twenty-nine of the thirty-nine cities. Both types of data covered grades two through seven. Changes over time were measured by a comparison of pretest and post-test average grade equivalent scores with each other and with the national norms. No control groups were available.

The data described above revealed that the reading scores of Title I students improved at an average rate approximating the normal rate for the average child (one month's improvement for each month of instruction). This improvement, if it is real and is representative of Title I schools, is much higher than the expected rate for low-income, central city schools. It was concluded that Title I reading projects appear to be having a positive effect on the reading achievement of educationally deprived children. Data from ten cities in arithmetic achievement showed gains nearly as large as those in reading.

An attempt was also made to measure the "holding power" (lowering of dropout rates) for Title I schools between 1965–1966 and 1966–1967. The data indicate that the dropout rate decreased by five percentage points in the two years, a trend "not apparent" in schools outside the target areas. Attendance was also reported to have increased in Title I schools in the second of the two years.

This particular evaluation suffers from a host of weaknesses, many of which were not under the control of the investigator. Some of the major problems are biased samples, noncomparable data with respect to grade levels, measures and test intervals, and lack of control groups with which to make comparisons. These shortcomings make any valid conclusions about the impact of the program problematic. Dentler

(1969, p. 33), reviewing the section of USOE's Title I/Year II dealing with large central cities, is pointed in his criticisms:

> The evidence concerning the first two years of
> Title I operations in big-city schools, limited as it is,
> suggests that programs designed to bring children to
> reading competency, and funded under conditions
> characteristic of Title I are of indeterminate educa-
> tional value. Most of the evidence is too unreliable
> to enable conclusions to be reached, and most of the
> evaluation designs employed fail to specify instruc-
> tional inputs in ways that would enable the analyst to
> infer the causes of outputs. Such carefully designed
> evaluations as have been executed indicate, moreover,
> that big-city Title I projects seldom modify conven-
> tional teaching practices sufficiently to result in either
> significant or enduring gains in student reading achieve-
> ment.[3]

A more comprehensive evaluation attempt for the third year was undertaken by the Evaluation Design Unit of the Bureau of Elementary and Secondary Education at USOE. This evaluation is currently scheduled for publication in 1969. It will be an assessment at the national level, with the unit of analysis the individual child, not the school or school system (Jaeger 1969). Based on a survey instrument, the assessment represents an attempt to circumvent some of the problems en-countered in the second year evaluation. In conducting the survey, USOE has three objectives: (1) to describe the types

---

[3]From the evidence we have been able to examine bearing on Title I evaluations at the local level, it seems that the great-est number have been conducted in the New York City school district by the Center for Urban Education, New York City. There have been at least sixty such studies conducted to date. Our review of twenty-four of these documents reveals that an over-all consistent positive effect on both cognition and atti-tude has not been found. This conclusion is consistent with that of Dentler (1969, p. 32), who reports that CUE investiga-tions have indicated an over-all failure of Title I.

of students receiving Title I aid in terms of academic need, economic need, and racial composition, i.e., to determine how efficient Title I is in providing educational services to disadvantaged children. The survey appears to be providing reliable descriptive information of this type. (2) To specify the ways in which the funds are being spent—the types of services provided. The major emphasis during the third year appears to have been on improving reading skills, with considerable effort also directed toward arithmetic and language achievement. (3) To obtain data on the effectiveness of the program in producing measurable educational benefits during 1967–1968. Little systematic evidence is available on this crucial question because Title I, which provides bloc grants to school districts for a multiplicity of purposes, is difficult to evaluate carefully (Jaeger 1969, p. 1). The survey on which the evaluation is based was conducted on a random sample of 465 school districts out of the 13,000 receiving Title I aid. Data were obtained from 3,300 principals and 26,000 elementary school teachers, who reported on 123,000 students. High response rates were obtained over all: some data were obtained on each district in the sample. Teachers were the primary sources of information on variables such as socioeconomic background of the students' families and parental expectations for their children's educational attainment.

The critical question of how effective Title I was in producing positive results (that is, in increasing achievement level and cognitive skills of children) in 1967–1968 cannot be answered conclusively because of the lack of grade equivalence scores for different school districts and within districts. The survey results are restricted to reading achievement scores on parallel tests administered to students at the beginning and end of the academic year. If data are available on at least 500 pupils for a given parallel test pair, they are being analyzed as a measure of the effectiveness of reading programs. Usable longitudinal data are available for only 11,700 students, or 12 percent of those in the national 1968 survey. A preliminary analysis by the USOE staff indicates that this percentage is not representative of the national sample. However, a systematic attempt is being made to compare post-treatment with pre-treatment scores for Title I students and to compare them with the scores of nonparticipants. Four groups are being used for comparison purposes: participating high gainers and low gainers and nonparticipating high gainers and low gainers. A comment by the chief of the Evaluation Design Unit of the Bureau of Elementary and Secondary Education, USOE, best summarizes the problems inherent in trying to assess the educational impact of this highly diversified, broad-ranging, blanket-coverage program: "A major institution of our society, which has been essentially unaccountable to its clients for over 200 years, cannot be expected to mend its ways overnight" (Jaeger 1969, p. 1).

Upward Bound

This program is under the auspices of the Office of Economic Opportunity (OEO). It started on a nationwide basis after an experimental summer program showed that provision of a precollege experience for selected disadvantaged children had some promise of success. In its first year of full-scale operation, which began in June of 1966, 215 educational institutions were involved. Upward Bound projects were established in most of the fifty states. There were approximately 20,000 secondary school students enrolled in the initial program, and by 1969 the number of participating institutions was about 300, with 26,000 pupils enrolled.

Colleges and universities or secondary schools with residential facilities run Upward Bound projects through cooperative arrangements with high school and community action programs. The program is designed to identify as potential college students high school students who would be overlooked by routine school procedures. The recruitment guidelines set forth by the federal government emphasize the use of a diverse source of recommendations, including former Upward Bound students, neighborhood groups, and clergy. It also specifies that OEO-financed Upward Bound students must come from families whose annual incomes are below the poverty line.

The program usually recruits students during their sophomore and junior years of high school. Once recruited, they remain in the program through the summer following their senior year of high school. It has as its objectives supplying sustained support and encouragement to the participants, motivating them to seek higher education, and helping them maintain college aspirations. It attempts to generate the necessary motivation and, where needed, to develop the basic skills necessary for the successful pursuit of a college education. There has been some effort to involve parents of the enrollees in Upward Bound through adult education programs, discussion groups, and advisory conferences.

The "treatment" usually takes the form of intensive summer and after-school contact in tutorial programs and enrichment activities and meetings with both secondary school and college faculty members. One of the goals is to establish a relationship between the enrollee and one specific college campus, both with respect to its personnel and facilities. The program has as an integral part of its design "sponsoring" colleges, and almost all of the enrollees spend some time, usually during the summer, in residence on the campus of a sponsoring institution.

The routine through which this acquaintance with a college takes place is fairly well established. However, the process through which high school students are to be motivated and their areas of difficulty identified and alleviated are primarily under the jurisdiction of the local program administration. This autonomy is intended to allow flexibility in meeting the particular needs of the individual project's population. Few restrictions are placed on a sponsoring institution's curriculum and program design, and thus each project serves its population in a unique way. Although the program does not provide support for students once they enter college, the Upward Bound staff is expected to help them gain admission to a postsecondary institution and to assist them in finding appropriate financial support.

During FY 1969 the cost of the program to the federal government was almost $31 million, or about 80 percent of its total cost. The national average is $1,200 per student per year of participation.

There are a limited number of studies of Upward Bound available,[4] and most do not present evaluation data; that is, much of their information is in the form of rhetoric. One simple criterion of the success of the program is the proportion of its participants who enroll in college. This assertion is frequently found in the literature: 80 percent enroll in a college. Slightly over 50 percent of the college entrants remain there, which is approximately the national retention rate (Shea 1967; Froomkin 1968; Gardenhire 1968; Kornegay 1968a). This does not, of course, indicate anything about the quality of the institutions in which Upward Bound students enroll or the conditions under which they are being retained. For example, one study has shown that most Upward Bound students go to predominantly black southern institutions (Kornegay 1968b), and it is possible that such students elsewhere have received special concessions.

The attempt to measure changes in perceptions and attitudes at some date after a participant enters a program has been made, and little change has been seen. Two important studies of the impact of the program on attitudinal variables and on achievement itself have been conducted by Hunt and Hardt (1968) and the American College Testing Program (1968). Neither research design, however, could be considered rigorous.

The Hunt and Hardt series of three studies focuses on attitudinal, perceptual, and achievement changes of high school students during enrollment in the Upward Bound program. Attitudinal measures purported to predict success in college with some accuracy showed small but statistically significant changes in Upward Bound students in comparison with a control group. Their high school grade point averages, however, did not change.

---

[4]Summaries of several evaluation studies prepared by Data Systems Office, Educational Associates, Inc., in its Semi-Annual Report to the Office of Economic Opportunity (December, 1968) have provided most of the information about evaluation. They were supplemented by a number of issues of the journal Idea Exchange, a publication of Educational Associates dealing with Upward Bound news.

Posner (1968, p. 25) notes that in several Upward Bound projects intensive summer work designed to raise academic performance has been followed by a decrease in the participants' grade point averages during the following regular school year. He offers as one explanation for this anomalous finding the suggestion that perhaps teachers "punish" students whose academic interest has been stimulated to the point where they no longer are able to tolerate a rather stultifying classroom situation.[5]

In sum, there have been few published evaluations of Upward Bound. However, a comprehensive evaluation at the national level is being conducted by Educational Associates, Inc., using "hard data," scheduled for completion some time in 1969 (personal communication from the chief of data systems, EAI, Washington, D.C.). Such evaluation as there is suggests that the program is successful as far as getting participants enrolled in college is concerned. Nevertheless, definitive conclusions would require comparisons with a control group. Evidence based on standardized measures of academic performance of enrollees in college is lacking.

---

[5] Another explanation is that Upward Bound students are more likely to change into more academically demanding high school programs, such as a college preparatory curriculum.

3. DESCRIPTION AND ANALYSIS OF SELECTED LOCAL PROGRAMS

The second part of our discussion of the two categories of intervention response deals with selected local compensatory programs. We have chosen eleven such programs and have considered the importance, the extent of success, the population served, and the methods employed in each case. We make no claim that this has eliminated the arbitrariness of the decision to include or exclude a program. Our intent is to illustrate the types of programs subsumed under the broad rubric of compensatory education.

In order to present this information in a readily comprehensible manner, these selected programs are summarized in the table below. To give a detailed profile of the rationale, design, and outcome of the programs summarized in the table lies beyond the province of this volume. We have made a few comments concerning the range of these programs which, we think, will also put compensatory programs in general in the proper perspective.

Size of target population for the various programs ranged from over sixty thousand students per year in Higher Horizons to fewer than twenty-five in the first year of the Bereiter-Engelmann program.

Cost per pupil was not available for every program, yet what figures there are indicate that the lower boundary is zero; that is, no expenditure above and beyond the usual school expenses (as in the Banneker project). At the higher end of the range would be the Perry Preschool Project, whose annual cost per pupil ran to approximately fifteen hundred dollars. Other programs may have cost even more, especially when funding came from several outside sources.

The highest intensity level probably occurred in the Bereiter-Engelmann program. There two time segments of the daily schedule were set aside for each child to receive instruction. During that time, with almost drill-like precision, he was bombarded with cognitive materials. In other programs cognitive material was not even presented directly but rather was assumed to be pervasive, perhaps even unnoticed on the pupil's part, as in the Banneker project.

Comparisons made to assess the progress of the experimental groups differ considerably in rigor and sophistication. Banneker reports comparisons with schools having a Negro population of 10 percent or less and with schools having a Negro population of 90 percent or more within the same school system. These data are kept by school systems as a matter of routine, regardless of their interest in compensatory education programs. Other programs attempted more detailed and rigorous comparisons, using control groups. On occasion, the control groups themselves were subject to bias, as, for example, those of the Institute for Developmental Studies in New York. The attrition rates in the schools in which the Institute's program was based have been so great that the evaluation has been jeopardized. The most elaborate use of control groups appears to be in the Peabody Early Training Project, in which 61 children were randomly assigned to one of two treatment groups (differing in length of exposure) or to a control group. In addition, a comparable, distal control group some sixty miles away served as a check on diffusion effects (see Chapter 5 below).

Types of treatment varied from the total immersion used in the Perry Preschool Project to the ancillary aid of Homework Helpers, who provided assistance outside of the classroom to elementary students.

Length of exposure ranged from a low of six to eight weeks in a summer Head Start program to a high of three or four years, as in More Effective Schools.

In the Early Training Project parental involvement was high; weekly home visits extended the program's influence to the home. In the Homework Helpers Program, on the other hand, to the best of our knowledge, no parental contact was involved.

Eleven Compensatory Education Programs

Title, Beginning Date, and Location	Maturational Level of Target Population	Objectives	Methods	Cognitive Gains[a]
Banneker, 1957, St. Louis, Mo.	Preschool through junior high	Achievement improvement; motivation of pupils; improvement of aspirational levels and self-concept; raising of teacher expectations	Exposure to successful adults; teacher in-service training; parental involvement; creation of heightened commitment to school through rallies and inter-scholastic competition	Three years after program terminated, reading test scores of schools involved were compared first with initial scores and then with those of other schools of similar racial and ethnic composition in the same school system; there was no significant gain in decreasing discrepancy in achievement between test schools and all-white schools in the same school system
Higher Horizons, 1959, New York City (This program was terminated in 1962.)	Elementary through junior high	Motivation of students and parents for higher achievement and educational plans	In-service teacher training to raise expectations and ability to teach these students; use of curriculum and guidance specialists to increase student motivation; enrichment programs; parental involvement; use of program volunteers; use of special remedial teachers to improve language and arithmetic skills	Data gathered at different times revealed no significant differences in reading and arithmetic scores between (1) experimental and control schools and (2) between experimental and control students matched on I.Q. and/or earlier achievement test scores

Program	Level	Objective	Methods	Results
More Effective Schools, 1964, New York City	Preschool through elementary	Identification and prevention of learning problems; creation of a responsive school climate	Team teaching; reduction of pupil-teacher ratio; teacher training; remedial curriculum features; cultural enrichment; parental involvement	No significant improvement noted in median reading achievement scores for fourth grade students who had been in the program for three years; no appreciable differences in levels of reading retardation between experimental and control schools comparable in ethnic composition
Early Training Project, 1959, Peabody College, Nashville, Tenn.	Preschool	Preparation of the disadvantaged to cope with and gain positively from learning situation in regular school	Summer school program; home visitors during rest of year; parental involvement; reinforcement for "correct" behavior; learning of concepts on abstract levels	Small but statistically significant differences in I.Q. noted between experimental and control groups after three summers of intervention and three years of home visitation; superiority in reading readiness scores for experimental groups two and a half years after program was initiated (experimental and control groups were formed by random assignment in this program)
Bereiter-Engelmann Academic Preschool Program, 1964, Champaign, Ill.	Preschool	Raising of achievement levels in reading, verbal, and numerical skills	Teacher training; special curriculum based on task analysis; parental involvement	Experimental groups showed significantly greater gains in I.Q., reading, and arithmetic than control groups at end of first and second years (experimental and control groups were formed by random assignment in this program)

Eleven Compensatory Education Programs—Cont'd.

Title, Beginning Date, and Location	Maturational Level of Target Population	Objectives	Methods	Cognitive Gains[a]
Institute for Developmental Studies, 1958, New York City	Preschool through third grade	Development of language and concept formation skills; prevention of deficiencies	Cultural enrichment; teacher in-service training; parental involvement; special materials and curricula	Inconsistent results obtained on both I.Q. and reading achievement tests in comparisons of experimental and control groups over time[b]
Perry Preschool Project, 1962, Ypsilanti, Mich.	Preschool	Improvement of language and numerical skills	Parental involvement; cultural enrichment; low pupil-teacher ratio; group teaching emphasizing verbal "bombardment," interaction, and dramatic play; home tutoring of parents	Significant I.Q. differences between experimental and control groups were noted at end of first year which were not maintained at three later points in time ("fade-out" effect). This pattern held for four other waves of students. Significant differences were seen between experimental and control groups (for all waves combined) in California Achievement Tests (experimental and control groups were formed by random assignment in this program)

Program	Level	Objective	Method	Results
Computer Assisted Instruction, 1964, Stanford University, Stanford, Calif.	Elementary	Improvement of basic reading and mathematics achievement	"Tutorial" and "drill-and-practice" approaches to individualized instruction. The former involves interaction of student and computer, based on a series of levels, each containing several lessons. Each lesson is constructed according to an instructional logic having the capability of "branching" contingent on the student's response. The second approach lacks the branching capability of the tutorial system	Early results showed significant differences in reading achievement and mathematics between experimental and control groups using the tutorial approach. (Experimental and control groups were formed by assigning half the subjects to CAI reading instruction and half to CAI math instruction. Thus the control group for reading was the group receiving math instruction, and vice versa.) Later experiments, however, have produced mixed results with control groups, which sometimes achieved significantly higher than the experimental groups. Evaluation of drill-and-practice approach shows mixed results; positive results were mostly with slow learners
Diagnostically Based Curriculum for Pre-School Deprived Children, 1964, Bloomington, Ind.	Preschool	Removal of deficits in language, motor coordination, and concept formation	Conventional preschool techniques conducted in highly structured settings; frequent field trips coordinated with classroom curriculum; continuous monitoring of each student's progress and needs	Significant differences in I.Q. and language development were obtained between experimental and control groups at end of one year for three different waves of subjects

Eleven Compensatory Education Programs—Cont'd.

Title, Beginning Date, and Location	Maturational Level of Target Population	Objectives	Methods	Cognitive Gains[a]
Homework Helpers,[c] 1963, New York City	High school[d]	Encouragement of high school tutors of elementary students to remain in school and achieve at higher levels through year-round efforts and economic incentives	High school tutors trained by master teachers, with daily supervision and guidance and frequent workshops using special curriculum materials; year-round efforts using economic incentives for tutors	Selection of tutors and nontutors was on a random basis of eligible participants (97 tutors, 57 controls); experimental group achieved significantly higher increases in reading on Iowa Silent Reading Tests than controls. However, no relationship was found between reading scores and performance in classroom
Small Group Basic Education Program, 1965,[e] Albion, Penn.	High school	Improvement of achievement in reading, mathematics, and writing; increase in school attendance; enhancement of self-esteem	Remedial curriculum; group and individual instruction; individual and group counseling; home visiting	Students selected for low performance in reading and math from low-income families. Experimental group did not increase significantly on Metropolitan Achievement Tests in either reading or math during a four-month period (no evidence of use of a control group)

[a] Based on data from standardized tests.

[b] See Hawkridge, Chalupsky, and Roberts (1968, Pt. 2, pp. 53–59) for a description of problems in evaluating the results. Their analysis for the period 1963–1968 did not yield "any clearly distinguishable results" (p. 54). However, a more recent report by Deutsch (1968) shows significant differences between experimental and control groups in reading achievement. Nevertheless, attrition rates in both groups were substantial, and several comparisons were made between experimental and "self-selected" control groups (pp. 102–4).

[c] This program was brought to our attention by Posner (1968).

[d] Evaluated only for high school students' performance, i.e., students employed as tutors for elementary and junior high school students.

[e] This program was brought to our attention by Hawkridge, Tallmadge, and Larsen (1968).

We hope that these comments have provided the reader with some idea of the diversity in the programs represented in the table and in the area as a whole, and with a clearer picture of the dangers of making generalizations about such programs. It is clear that the results of these various approaches to compensatory education are ambiguous with respect to raising the I.Q. and/or the achievement level of disadvantaged children. Almost all of the programs manifest awareness of the interpretative bias which can occur when the evaluation of a program is limited to a summary test score. At the same time, it is recognized that these types of tests do reveal discrepancies in achievement levels when disadvantaged children compete in the usual classroom setting. Consequently, almost every compensatory educational program with a modicum of testing sophistication—and most of them have some connections with either colleges or public schools, where testing is an accepted practice—are at least able to report scores based on standardized intelligence or achievement tests. More important, the tests are readily available and are relatively easy to administer because of the work done by the researchers who attempted to standardize them.

The layman is at an advantage if he can use such existing tests. On the other hand, it is almost unrealistic to ask for socioemotional or attitudinal measures, and this statement is overwhelmingly true if it is left up to the project director to devise such measuring instruments. Thus, the controversy over compensatory education programs has come to revolve almost exclusively around scores on standardized intelligence and achievement tests. Small wonder that every report one reads, including those with the tightest experimental designs and evaluation procedures, cautions that the available statistical measures have reduced the project to so narrow a range that its success story cannot be fully told, and almost every one supplements the test scores with accounts of the enthusiasm for it expressed by parents—a "finding" which can be reported for almost any project.

Parental enthusiasm seems to be a universal finding in preschool programs, regardless of their duration, type, or reported results. However, we have found no indication as to whether this enthusiasm is just an extension of the faith most parents have in the larger school system (a faith which now seems to be on the decline), whether it is the Hawthorne effect, whether it is a mistaken belief that any extra help will lead automatically to gains in reading or arithmetic, or whether parents can detect small changes in their children which elude the tester. We do not know why parents (and often other observers) are enthusiastic, and thus the one finding which is always reported cannot be interpreted clearly.

4. EVALUATION RESEARCH AND "REALITY"

A set of recurring problems plagues the evaluator of the programs we have reviewed here and those discussed by other reviewers. It seems safe to conclude that many of them will persist for some time and therefore deserve discussion.

Immediate Evaluation

Pressures for immediate, as opposed to long-term, carefully planned evaluation will continue until major policy-makers feel that compensatory education programs have demonstrated their value. There is pressure not only for immediate but for successful social action. The variety of programs in existence and the urgent demand that each be evaluated quickly reflects a "try everything" philosophy (or, perhaps more accurately, "try anything"), a philosophy based on the hope that if enough experiments are instituted, something will work.

Perhaps demonstrated success on the part of one program (whether in the field of special education or not) will reduce the demand for quick results from others. At any rate, social reforms cannot be held in abeyance until social scientists can predict with reasonable accuracy whether a given approach will in fact be successful. To delay in this fashion would be to opt for one horn of the dilemma posed by Hawkridge and his associates: "Action and research are to some extent incompatible. The first seeks to guarantee a predetermined outcome; axiomatically it spares no effort and is entirely dependent upon the existing store of knowledge and information; time is of the essence. Research, on the other hand, is often slow; unless it deliberately and selectively restricts the scope of action it may seriously handicap the attempt to add new knowledge to the existing store" (Hawkridge, Chalupsky, and Roberts 1968, Pt. 1, p. 15).

This incompatibility may be partially a matter of differing role conceptions. The professional training of those who perform evaluation research is geared to the notion that research

45

takes time. The researcher strongly resists speed and time constraints. While there is no necessary connection between speedily executed and sloppy research, the evaluator may be disposed to see just such a connection and claim professional immunity from deadlines.

The pressure for immediate results does not create an atmosphere conducive to long-range planning with careful feedback from controlled programs. Some programs, of course, have been in effect for five years or more, yet if one takes the position that their true impact may be realized only when this generation of disadvantaged children become parents, long-term evaluation is dictated. A plausible argument could be made that the attitudes and approaches to child-rearing and education in the home which are being inculcated in these children will show up in larger incremental gains in the next generation. Such a consideration, however, remains in the realm of unanswerable speculation. It is the extreme response to the more reasonable question of how long we should invest in a program which shows tenuous or nonsignificant results before giving it up as of no value. The immediate need for effective programs will continue to exert pressure toward short-term evaluation.

Vagueness of Criteria

Current programs in compensatory education are handicapped by the vagueness with which each of their objectives is specified. This becomes increasingly true the younger the target population. With younger children fewer skills can be taught, and some educators are violently opposed to teaching any cognitive skills, such as reading—or its predecessor, reading readiness—to preschool children. All can agree on the objective of establishing a program which will make it easier for children to adjust successfully to regular school settings or to achieve within the conventional classroom scholastic performance consistently higher than is now obtained. However, when one is actually trying to evaluate the effectiveness of a compensatory education program, one finds it imperative that goals be specific enough to permit measurement. It is this which is truly difficult. Should only intelligence and/or achievement scores be used as the criterion, or should the more elusive variables of self-concept, teacher warmth, parental and community responsiveness, and a variety of other measures be considered? When the program is directed primarily toward parents or teachers, with the expectation that its effects will be transferred indirectly to the students, the problem is even more difficult. Exactly what is the real criterion of measurement when money is spent on teacher training programs or parental discussion groups? Does one still want to measure the impact on the student?

To insist on measuring only the effects of the program on students is to choose what Scriven (1967) has termed "pay-off evaluation"; that is, appraisal of pre- and post-test performance differences with a view to ascertaining what the program has done for the students. It is the "black box" technique once more, and has the attraction of simplicity. Scriven also discusses "intrinsic evaluation," wherein criteria are seldom operationalized and what is evaluated is the intrinsic worth of the program itself, not necessarily its effects. In this approach intermediate rather than final goals of the program are evaluated. Intrinsic evaluation would have the value of identifying those aspects of the program which were successful, despite possible over-all negative results. These successful segments could conceivably be salvaged for other programs in the hope that building a catalog of successful components would result eventually in a successful whole.

Since compensatory education programs are not immune to politics, it is frequently not an accident that their goals remain vague and imprecise. Negative evaluations have their political consequences, and if one can live with essentially unmeasurable objectives, the possibility of negative findings is precluded. This may be the case, for example, with such ambiguous objectives as "cultural enrichment." One may easily identify possible methods of "cultural enrichment"—field trips, visits to museums and public buildings, summer camps, etc.— yet each person would be hard put to find an adequate measure of cultural enrichment. Still, it remains a stated objective of many compensatory education programs.

47

If vagueness of goals is the bane of the evaluation researcher, it may be the salvation of the program administrator. Frequently, in the face of imprecise objectives, the evaluator finds that he must make the criteria operationally specific. He does so as best he can and proceeds with his research. Should he produce findings which are unflattering to the program, any of its proponents (from senator to superintendent, from concerned parent to involved teacher) can attack him on the grounds that the "true objectives" of the program were not understood (Rossi 1969). There is the same kind of utility in having multiple objectives. If an evaluator declares that the program has failed to fulfill one objective, its defendants can then stress the importance of the ones that were not measured. If one's goals are not specified at the beginning of a program, the freedom to announce them at some later date is pretty well assured and serves as a political safety measure.

Treatment Modification

Because we lack knowledge in the area of child development and learning and because each program is aimed at the needs of individual participants, it is not at all uncommon to find that its approach was changed before adequate evaluation had been made.[1] Under such circumstances, one must face the question of what treatment is being researched.

Often modification of a program is beyond the control of either the evaluator or the program administrators. The Higher Horizons program in New York, for example, was not fully implemented until a demonstration project indicated success. When it was implemented, Higher Horizons was not funded at the level originally planned, and curtailment of its scope and method was necessary. It could not be evaluated in terms of the original plans, for they were not realized. One could, of course, evaluate it as it stood, but the question of

---

[1] For example, Deutsch (1968, p. 107) considered the first two groups of his subjects as comprising pilot waves because of this problem.

"what might have been" could never be answered. A clear statement of procedures and objectives would be of no help in this case, for the political facts of the matter made scientific norms irrelevant.

The conception of evaluation implicitly adopted in our review has been what Scriven (1967) calls "summative," that is, evaluation of the end product of a program. In part, this conception has been necessitated by the manner in which we posed our questions initially. Scriven also argues for "formative" evaluation—evaluation that is built into the process of developing a program. This kind of research is exemplified by both the Early Training Project at Peabody College and the Institute for Developmental Studies in New York.

Which Treatment?

Singling out people for special attention has been shown to affect their behavior. It is the well-known Hawthorne effect. If compensatory education programs achieve improvement initially, it may be that the treatment itself has had little to do with the gain and that any special attention to the enrollees would have achieved the same results. The potential presence of a Hawthorne effect makes it hazardous to generalize results or to try to replicate them in another setting. Of course, creative and imaginative variations of simple experimental designs for certain compensatory education efforts, such as the Stanford Computer Assisted Instruction Program, can help eliminate some of the factors which produce the Hawthorne effect. The Stanford sample of students was divided into two groups, with half receiving CAI reading instruction and the other half receiving CAI math instruction. Thus curriculum effects could be tested in two fields with only two groups, while the Hawthorne effect was minimized.

From a larger perspective, however, the Hawthorne effect, which is a nuisance to the evaluator, may be a boon to the program, and once again one can see a point at which the aims of programs may conflict with those of evaluation researchers. Typically, the Hawthorne effect means that subjects become enthusiastic when they know they are receiving special attention. The evaluation researcher wishes to minimize a Hawthorne effect because it obscures the real treatment effects of the program. However, these programs are designed to promote learning, and no one would argue that enthusiasm is dysfunctional for the learning process.

Scarce Resources

In addition to program modification and Hawthorne effects, there are other factors mitigating against the replicability of a successful approach to which attention should be given. The cost of a program obviously affects its scope. Some difficulties can arise from lack of funds to implement a program at the level planned, as in Higher Horizons, or the way in which funds are allocated may preclude any evaluation at all along rigorous scientific lines. School administrators who are quite willing to receive the benefits of compensatory education programs are sometimes unwilling to have those benefits evaluated. Posner (1968) suggests that this was the case with Ford Foundation's Great Cities program.

Money for evaluation research is scarce. Every dollar spent for evaluation is in some sense a dollar taken away from the operation of the program, and compensatory education may be expected to swing between two poles. At first, the demand is for action, and evaluation is neglected. Later, however, when the question of re-appropriating funds arises, more attention and resources will be devoted to evaluation. Pressure for evaluation may also arise when important public figures and/or the mass media accuse a program of failure.

A second scarce resource is rare skills, as in the Crisis Teachers program, the success of which depends largely upon its specially trained teachers. Similarly, a pilot or demonstration project always receives an extra amount of enthusiasm and hard work (a Hawthorne effect among administrators). This effect, which we call that of the "charismatic innovator," will frequently disappear when the project is exported or disseminated to other less dedicated persons who have not been affected by the charisma of the originator. Typically, a dynamic director, the charismatic innovator, will begin a limited project. The project will receive attention because of its purported dramatic effects. School officials wish to see it expanded, and it is here that problems of scale may arise. While the original treatment is always restricted in scope, there is a temptation to make generalizations over a broader range than the data warrant. For example, class size may be reduced to ten pupils in a demonstration project, significant results are found, and it is concluded that a reduced pupil-teacher ratio is the determining factor. This may not be quite true. We do not know whether reducing class size from twenty-five to twenty has anything like the effect of reducing class size from twenty to ten. There may be certain critical levels below which pupil-teacher ratio makes a difference and above which it does not.

Again, when seemingly successful programs are extended to a much larger group, administrative problems of the educational bureaucracy not encountered in the smaller experimental situation may have ludicrous consequences. In a recent conversation with us, an investigator actively involved in evaluation research reported that when evaluators asked teachers for an opinion as to the success of a program being conducted in their school, the frequent response was: "What program?" Apparently they were aware that one or two new wrinkles had been added to their daily routines, but many had no idea that they were principal agents in a compensatory education program with a specific set of objectives. Somehow this fact had never been effectively communicated to them through the bureaucracy.

Test Situations

Several instances have been cited in which initial gains in experimental groups failed to be retained over time. There are several explanations as to why this "fadeout" phenomenon occurs, but it has not yet been studied in sufficient detail for the question to be answered definitively.[2]

---

[2] We have touched upon this subject earlier (see pp. 7–10 above).

Current explanations, however, center around the test situation itself. To be sure, when an individual has scored particularly low on the tests, then the measurement is likely to be an underestimate of his true ability. Test theory predicts that without any increase in knowledge a subject's observed score would be higher on a second test. The problem is one of ascertaining, when scores are particularly low on a first test and higher on a retest, how much of the increase is due to the regression phenomenon and how much is due to the treatment effect.

Observed gains may be accounted for in another manner. How much improvement can come from simple exposure to and practice in the test-retest situation? It seems a fair assumption that in most preschool educational intervention programs the subject has never before experienced a testing situation. Test theory would predict some amount of improvement simply on the basis that the child has practice in taking the test. It would appear to us, however, that this phenomenon could be controlled by testing the child several times in the pretest period. Test familiarity would be assured for all subjects at the beginning of the program, and post-tests would be more likely to reflect true gains. Another strategy is suggested by Kagan (1969), based on Palmer's research: "each examiner was instructed not to begin any testing with any child until she felt that the child was completely relaxed, and understood what was required of him. Many children had five, six, and even seven hours of rapport sessions with the examiner before any questions were administered" (p. 276). However, awareness of the importance of the test situation does not seem, unfortunately, to be widespread among data collectors.[3]

_____

[3]For example, in a recent evaluation of a summer Head Start project, Chorost et al. (1967) discovered gains during the summer experience followed by the fadeout effect during the formal school year. They speculate that the initial scores on the tests were uncharacteristically low because the students were emotionally unprepared for the testing experience, in

Finally, in working with children at the preschool and elementary levels, in almost all cases adults play a greater role in administering tests than in programs for older children. The administrator of the test can have a contaminating effect, particularly with this target population. At the very least, he represents one additional variable in the test situation: some tests, for example, have to be administered orally, since the preschool child cannot read. Such unintentional effects contaminate the test situation, so that uniformity of testing from one setting to another becomes the ideal rather than a reality.

Awareness of these problems should focus our efforts on the creation of uniform test situations for preschool populations.

Control Groups

Several problems center around the use of control groups. Experimental design dictates the use of randomly selected and assigned experimental and control groups, but problems arise in connection with achieving this goal. Even though an evaluation design dictates the use of control groups, it may not be in the power of the experimenter to exclude any subject from the program. If the control group receives no help, this decision is sometimes viewed as a form of discrimination. The legislation for Title I programs provides an example: "Title I evaluation, however, is not amenable to strict experimental conditions. All educationally disadvantaged children are included in designed projects. It is not the intent of the legislation to withhold help from disadvantaged children for experimental or research reasons. A child is included or excluded . . . not on the basis of a sophisticated sampling procedure" (Title I/Year II, p. 126). Hence the goals of democratic administration override the scientific goals of evaluation.

---

which strangers were used as administrators. It is noteworthy that a control group, which would have provided some evidence to support or refute this speculation, was not used in this study.

In other cases, even where the situation allows a part of the population to receive no treatment or a different treatment, there is still the problem of intact groups. Randomization of control and experimental groups is impeded by the natural indivisibility of school classes or neighborhoods. When control and experimental groups are in close proximity to each other—which is the usual case—one group can be contaminated by the other. Although the problem is usually thought of in terms of the experimenter's contaminating the control group, it is also true that the control group itself can neutralize some of the effects of the experiment, as we suggested earlier.[4] In a peer play situation, standard English could be strongly condemned; in a school situation a teacher might inadvertently handle both experimental and control groups in a like manner.

Curiously, contaminations which are detrimental to evaluation attempts may be unintentionally beneficial to the program objective. The Early Training Project at Peabody College suggests that there may be "horizontal" contamination—that the interaction of control and experimental groups in the neighborhood may explain the finding that the scores of the control group also increased. These researchers are also investigating "vertical" contamination, in which siblings of children in the experimental group showed gains on test scores. In addition, when programs are aimed at parents, effects may spread from mother to mother as another form of contamination. All of these are discussed in the Early Training Project (Klaus and Gray 1968). In terms of achieving over-all program objectives, such contamination is a windfall, however it may complicate the task of the evaluator.[5]

---

[4] See p. 10 above.

[5] Again, vis-à-vis potential contradictions between program objectives and evaluation objectives, although this phenomenon is an unintentional occurrence, it would seem to be desirable from the standpoint of the program and undesirable to the evaluator, who seeks a research design which assures uncontaminated or "clean" control groups.

5. CONCLUSIONS

Strategies for Success in Compensatory Education

The evidence regarding the effectiveness of compensatory education is ambiguous. We, like Posner (1968, p. ii) and Hawkridge, Chalupsky, and Roberts (1968),[1] discovered few projects which demonstrated persistent and consistent results. However, it is debatable whether this ambiguity is a consequence of the inadequacy of the programs or of the evaluations, for little of the evidence has been obtained from tightly conceived research designs and adequate samples, testing, and data interpretation. This conclusion regarding the effectiveness of compensatory education is more guarded than that of the U.S. Civil Rights Commission (1967), which has taken the position that because in the period 1957–1966 none of the programs focused on Negro students in primarily Negro schools appeared to have significantly increased the achievement of participating students as a group (p. 138), future programs conducted in racially and socially isolated environments are not likely to succeed.[2] It should be noted, however, that the Civil Rights Commission staff reviewed only approximately twenty programs.

---

[1]Hawkridge and his associates (Pt. 1, p. 11) conducted a literature and mail search of over a thousand compensatory education programs and discovered only approximately a hundred which met the following criteria: (a) the program report was completed in 1963 or later; (b) the program was directed toward disadvantaged children at the preschool, elementary, or secondary level; (c) the enrollees gained in cognitive achievement, with the primary focus upon reading or language arts, mathematics, or I.Q.; and (d) the program showed evidence of experimental design good enough to justify some degree of confidence in the findings.

[2]However, one cannot conclude from the present evidence that school desegregation per se or compensatory education in desegregated settings will significantly decrease the sizable

Despite the ambiguity of results and the paucity of documentation regarding compensatory education, there are strategies which should be carefully considered. A comparison of "successful" and "unsuccessful" programs has been conducted by Hawkridge, Tallmadge, and Larsen (1968), and another less ambitious, yet highly informative study was made by Posner (1968). The recommendations emanating from these two studies are quite congruent and are generally consistent with the observations and suggestions of a variety of persons concerned with compensatory education; for example, journalists (Pines 1967), experts in human learning (Jensen 1969), and the academicians who developed some of the more widely acclaimed compensatory programs (Bereiter 1967).

The specific objective of the Hawkridge project was to identify the factors most frequently associated with successful and with unsuccessful programs. "Successful" programs resulted in cognitive gains (as measured by standardized tests) significantly greater for students in the program than for those

---

discrepancy in average achievement between Negroes and whites. For example, as Nichols (1968) notes, the evidence in the Commission report does not demonstrate unequivocally that there is a significant relationship between the racial composition of schools and the achievement of Negroes. In this connection, Posner (1968, pp. 7–15) cites longitudinal evidence from the compensatory education program in racially balanced schools in Hartsdale, New York. Despite the fact that achievement scores on standardized tests increased for both Negroes and whites between 1961 and 1965, the initial differences between the two groups favoring the whites actually increased. There are a number of other studies which strongly suggest facilitative effects of desegregation on the achievement of Negro students. (For a summary and bibliography of research in this area, see Weinberg 1968). Given our present state of knowledge of the teaching-learning process and the magnitude of our educational crisis, the most defensible policy prescription is that advocated by Harold Howe: "We must pursue both compensatory education and desegregated schools at the same time" (1967, p. 776).

in conventional school programs. "Unsuccessful" programs were defined as those which, although well designed, failed to yield cognitive gains. The two types of programs were matched as closely as possible with regard to similarity of objectives and age of students. Ethnic composition of students, types of learning involved, and number of students were considered when feasible. The programs were then analyzed in terms of ninety-one components, and the similarities and differences between the successful and unsuccessful programs were noted in both qualitative and quantitative terms. The results were not scientifically conclusive in the strict sense. However, meaningful patterns did emerge which warrant careful consideration in the planning, execution, and evaluation of future compensatory education efforts.

In the Posner study, fifteen successful compensatory programs were investigated in an attempt to identify the features that made for success. Three criteria were used in selecting the programs: (a) the quality of the research design and evidence of objective results persisting over time, as defined by experienced observers of compensatory education efforts; (b) objectives differing from those of other programs selected; and (c) accessibility of programs for site visits.

In neither study do the authors claim that their samples are representative of all successful or unsuccessful compensatory education programs. However, it is our conviction that these two studies are among the most important to date.[3] Hawkridge, Tallmadge, and Larsen (1968) found that the following characteristics most clearly distinguished successful from unsuccessful efforts and formed their policy recommendations accordingly: (a) careful planning and clear statement of academic objectives; (b) small groups and a high degree of individualization of instruction; (c) instruction and materials that were relevant and were closely linked to program objectives;

---

[3] This statement refers only to studies comparing several compensatory programs.

(d) high intensity of treatment; and (e) teacher training in the methods of the program.[4]

Some of Posner's more important recommendations are as follows: (a) objectives should be clearly defined and systematic procedures and time schedules for the implementation of plans should be set up; (b) instruction should be individualized by various means such as one-to-one relationships between teachers and students, tutorial sessions, and computer-assisted instruction; (c) funds should be allocated at all maturational levels—preschool, elementary, and secondary—and should not be concentrated at the preschool level to the extent of shortchanging elementary and secondary programs, since some of the more successful pay-offs have been achieved with students who are more mature chronologically. (The Homework Helpers program in New York City, which showed gains in reading skills for both disadvantaged adolescent tutors and their elementary school pupils, is an excellent example of positive results at costs much lower than many other highly publicized programs).

Perhaps the best approach to discussion of these recommendations is to summarize two programs which we believe to be outstanding examples of successful innovative ventures in compensatory education. One is the Bereiter-Engelmann Academic Preschool Program, originating at the Institute for Research on Exceptional Children, University of Illinois. The objectives of the program were to teach language, reading, and arithmetic skills to preschool children of low socioeconomic background, most of whom were Negroes. The students received equal amounts of instruction in each curriculum based on task analysis and programming of tasks (Bereiter and Engelmann 1966; Rusk 1969). Stated differently, the designers developed specific learning objectives and instructional methods

---

[4]In the Coleman survey (1966) the researchers found that teacher quality, as measured by educational level, verbal facility, and family educational background, was one of the most important school correlates of student performance on standardized tests.

to achieve these goals. These methods involved the specification of well-defined concepts and operations for each curriculum, with a heavy emphasis on constructions and intensive drills in predetermined sequences. Thus, for example, the language curriculum was based on the premise that the rules of language require understanding and generalizing of analogies and focused on dramatizing analogies. Concepts were grouped on the basis of the rules governing their manipulation rather than on thematic association (Hawkridge, Chalupsky, and Roberts 1968, Pt. 2, p. 117). Classes were conducted for two hours daily, five days a week, for the entire academic year. In the classroom sessions the students were told what they were supposed to learn, what the criteria of learning are, and the usefulness of the curriculum to the larger social world. This information was communicated through examples and careful control of teachers' responses. The students were taught in small, homogeneous groups (pupil-teacher ratio was 5 : 1) using a highly structured curriculum emphasizing cognitive growth, not socioemotional development. Teachers were carefully selected and intensively trained in the methods, rationale, and philosophy of the program. Finally, parental involvement was an important component of the program. Several meetings with parents were held in the course of the academic year to explain the program and to encourage them to accept preschool as a serious academic enterprise, not a "baby-tending" service (Bereiter and Engelmann 1966, p. 73).

Bereiter and Engelmann and others who have used this approach have consistently obtained measurable, positive results, which have been succinctly summarized by Rusk (1969). Three different cohorts of preschool students showed positive, significant cognitive gains over an academic year. The first group maintained its original gains during a kindergarten year, and the second group improved upon them. No control groups were used in the first year of the program; however, the second and third cohorts were part of a larger study conducted by Karnes (1968) involving five different approaches to preschool training. Karnes concluded that the two highly structured approaches—Bereiter-Engelmann's and hers—were more effective in enhancing and maintaining cognitive functioning than the other three. Even more important, however, was the fact that students in the Bereiter-Engelmann program did not suffer fadeout effects at the end of two years' exposure: their scores on tests of psycholinguistic abilities increased during the course of the second year.

Rusk's own research adds further support for the Bereiter-Engelmann "pressure-cooker" (Pines 1967) approach. The purpose of his investigation was to determine whether in a six-week summer curriculum, using the Bereiter-Engelmann method, Head Start children would make significant gains over students in a comparison group exposed to a more traditional, less structured approach. The pretest–post-test measures of concept acquisition for the two groups supported the conclusion that children in the academically oriented curriculum made significant cognitive gains over children in a less structured curriculum "emphasizing social objectives and the broadening of experience with the world" (Rusk 1969, p. 3). One of the most important aspects of Rusk's research is that these differences between the two groups were achieved during the course of a summer program. (The differences were attributed primarily to the differences in teacher-training programs.) Other researchers have doubted that summer compensatory programs last long enough to produce positive results, and Rusk acknowledges that in his particular study the fadeout effect noted in the follow-up studies of subjects in several other compensatory programs might be present. Only systematic longitudinal research can answer this crucial question.

From this brief description of the Bereiter-Engelmann program, it is evident that it contains (with one exception) the features which characterize all successful programs according to Hawkridge and associates and Posner. The exception involves Posner's recommendation that compensatory education funds should not be concentrated on any one age group: Bereiter and Engelmann have been classified as belonging to the "cognitive" school, which argues that disadvantaged children deprived of early intellectual stimulation are unlikely to fulfill later their academic potential. To this assumed disagreement it may be answered that the secondary school students in some of the successful programs described by Posner may not be disadvantaged to the extent of those in Bereiter's program;[5] further, it is generally acknowledged that at present both compensatory education programs and their evaluation are an art, not a science, and one cannot afford to reject promising experiments out of hand.

The Early Training Project at Peabody College is another example of a successfully conducted program which has been continually evaluated and revised in the quest for a practical and generalizable intervention program for disadvantaged children. The project was initially conceived in 1959, primarily to provide field experience to graduate students in a school psychology program at Peabody College in Nashville, Tennessee. However, the dearth of information about child development and the growing awareness of the need for such knowledge provided an incentive to expand the program.

The design was based on findings abstracted from the relevant literature in the behaviorial sciences, and attention was paid both to theory and to methodology. Pupils were randomly assigned to one of two experimental conditions (subjects participated in the summer program for differing lengths of time) or to a control group (local control group). A third group of students who lived some distance from the town in which the experiment was conducted was also included in the study as a second type of control group (distal control group). It was included to provide information on diffusion effects which might occur.

One of the treatment groups participated in the Early Training Project for the three summers before it entered first grade. The second treatment group participated for only two summers. The length of participation was the only intended difference between the two experimental groups. The goal of

----

[5] There is evidence to indicate that this is true. For example, in the Homework Helpers program, which both Hawkridge and Posner label as successful, the average reading level for both the experimental and control groups was roughly at the tenth grade. However, the ranges in both groups were substantial.

the program was to prevent the handicaps which many disadvantaged pupils experience in the conventional classroom. Several areas in which the children's behavior was to be modified or strengthened because of its relevance to success in regular school were specified. These variables, along with a short explanation of the basis on which they were chosen, are given below.

(a) Attitudes relating to achievement in school. (1) Motivation: beginning with play activities, pupils were exposed to a series of situations in which they could successfully compete. Through such rewarded and successful competition, the motivation to continue such striving and to value achievement positively was strengthened. (2) Delay of gratification: the children were given a number of opportunities to choose between having "a little now or more later" of items such as candy. At first the time between "now" and "later" was very short, but it was gradually increased as pupils learned that the additional reward did materialize. (3) Interest in activities related to school: many of the summer activities, as one would expect, involved books, stories, painting, and drawing, but books were also made available for family use in an effort to make a bridge between the activities the child participates in before and after he enters public school. (4) Identification with role models: there was frequent and intensive interaction between the children and the adult teachers and aides during the summer program. This was possible because of a high ratio of adults to pupils. An effort was also made to provide contact with males for children from homes in which the father was absent.

(b) Aptitudes for achievement in school. (1) Perceptual development: a good deal of time was spent in focusing the child's attention on similarities and differences in objects. Both auditory and visual discrimination, skills which are needed for coping with verbal and written language, were encouraged through this means. (2) Concept formation: these exercises consisted of classifying, reclassifying, and generalizing about objects. This emphasis is, of course, based on Piaget's theory of concrete operationalizing, which attempts to explain a child's intellectual development. (3) Language development: expression through verbalizing and play-acting was stressed. One of the problems faced by disadvantaged children is their lack of experience in verbalizing their thoughts in the usual sentence form expected by regular school teachers.

In order to maintain and strengthen any positive effects of the summer program, a trained project worker acted as a school-home liaison. On home visits he provided information and advice and acted as a resource person for parents when they sought help. The home visits were scheduled for forty-five minutes or more of each week that the summer program was inoperative. The idea was to stimulate the family to become a more effective educational agent for its children, mainly through work with mothers. A kind of training session for the mother was a vital part of this phase of the program. Concrete suggestions as to how they could help their children without interfering with the normal work or routine of the home were offered. Mothers were encouraged—and given practice through role-playing—to interact verbally with their children and to reward desirable behavior.

There were attempts to measure the success of the program in terms of psychological variables, such as those of achievement motivation and delay of gratification. These attempts proved to be rather unsuccessful. Many of the problems discussed in Chapter 1 above plagued the analysis of changes in the children's motivation and attitude toward school. Thus the success of this part of the program remains uncertain.

Although much of the work conducted in the program was focused on the child's attitudes and motivations, it was recognized that unless his academic performance in school was actually improved, its most important objective would not be achieved. Extensive testing was carried out from the very beginning of the project. A standard set of instruments was used to assess changes in school aptitude among the experimental and control groups. The numbers in the groups were small, but unlike the situation faced by the Institute for Developmental Studies, the attrition rate was very low. The maximum numbers for comparisons ranged from twenty to twenty-six pupils per group. The most frequent comparisons were between the two experimental groups combined and the two control groups combined. In addition, comparisons were made to test whether length of exposure to the program was a factor in differences between the two experimental groups. In a comparable manner, the local and distal control groups were compared to see whether any diffusion effects could be detected.

The Stanford-Binet I.Q. test, the Peabody Picture Vocabulary Test, and the Wechsler Intelligence Scale for Children all showed the same pattern: the two combined experimental groups significantly exceeded the two control groups in performance. However, neither longer participation in the program (three summers rather than two) nor diffusion (distal vs. local control) had a significant effect on the scores. The WISC was also analyzed by subtests. On seven out of ten subtests the performance of the combined experimental groups was significantly superior to that of the combined control groups.

The Illinois Test of Psycholinguistic Abilities was administered three times. The first two administrations (1964 and 1965) showed significant differences between experimental and control groups. There was a steady decline on each successive performance by the experimental groups, and by 1966, the children's second year in regular school, the experimental and control groups were performing at the same level.

The Metropolitan Readiness Tests and the Gates Reading Readiness Test were administered in 1964. Again there was no difference between the two experimental groups, but their combined performance was superior to that of the control groups combined. The experimental groups' performance was higher on ten of eleven of the subtests for the two series. There is some slight evidence that the local control group performed better than the distal control group, suggesting that there had been some positive diffusion from the program.

Two series of achievement tests, the Metropolitan Achievement Tests and Stanford Achievement Tests, were administered after the subjects had enrolled in a regular school program (1965 and 1966). The same pattern of experimental group superiority held for these tests. Closer inspection of the test results indicates that this superiority is accounted for by the fact that the distal control group's performance was lower than any of the three groups located in the town in which the program was administered. Such results could be explained on the basis of diffusion from experimental to local control group. However, there was not enough information reported to rule out alternative explanations, such as superiority of teaching staff or more active parental support.

We have some reservations concerning the diffusion explanation and concerning the combination of the two experimental and control groups for comparison purposes. From the data reported, it is difficult to see how the experimental groups performed significantly better than the local control group, since in most instances (eight out of twelve subtests, in the case of the Stanford Achievement Test) the local control group scored better than the experimental group that had been exposed longest to the program. In other words, we hesitate to conclude that the only cause (or even the most important cause) of these differences between the two control groups was the indirect impact of the program through diffusion. Second, combining the two control groups does make the superiority of the experimental groups consistent even after they have entered regular school, the time when many program staffs report fadeout effects or a failure to maintain initial gains. It is our belief that this would also be the case with the achievement scores reported here if it were not for the inclusion of the distal control group. If, after further study, this difference between distal and local control group performance indeed proves to be caused by diffusion, it will be one of the most encouraging findings thus far for everyone involved in preschool remedial instruction.

Strategies for Evaluation

It seems likely that funds will continue to be provided for compensatory education, as well as for other programs directed at the disadvantaged. The notion that innovation in education is self-justifying is becoming accepted in the United States (Posner 1968, p. 30), and the various poverty programs spawned in the last ten years or so have become an integral part of federal, state, and local governmental agencies. To eliminate them might not be politically feasible; they have gained a foothold in the bureaucracies (Moynihan 1969, pp. 156–57). Our future efforts should be aimed not at determining whether an entire program, such as Head Start, should be abolished because over all it is unsuccessful, for such programs are most likely here to stay. Rather, we should attempt to answer the question of which of the alternative methods appears most successful: for example, are year-round Head Start programs more effective than those lasting only for the summer?[6]

In compensatory education research we are still trying to diagnose the problems and their causes while simultaneously applying remedies. The society insists that we be receptive to the possibility of finding a workable solution even before we understand the mechanism by which that solution works. During World War II psychologists developed a successful method for screening potential navigators and fliers without knowing why it was successful (Guilford 1954, pp. 415–16). Only much later did researchers discover why the technique worked. Considerable flexibility is required, a flexibility incompatible with "scientific" evaluation in the strict sense. We are aware of the incompatibility, and, what is more, we approve of it.

The dilemma which we must live with is that of maximizing program flexibility while at the same time maximizing our

---

[6]Evidence from the recent Westinghouse study (Granger et al. 1969) indicates that full-year Head Start programs are superior to summer programs. It recommends that summer programs be converted into full-year or extended year programs.

knowledge of what is effecting change. Where evaluation research shows what will work and what will not, its recommendations should be utilized in program design. Where it shows little or nothing concerning the variables to be manipulated, we should learn from innovative programs that appear to have been successful. We shall return to this point below.

Some few programs have as part of their design evaluation procedures which are used to structure them in such a way as to effect the desired change (Scriven's "formative" evaluation; Scriven 1967). Such procedures can be invaluable and are all too few. We have observed that most projects with built-in evaluational mechanisms are based in universities.[7] In such cases, professionals' own careers are influenced by their discipline, which requires that the programs developed "work" and that it be known why they work. Academicians impose rather rigid standards on the work of their colleagues, and while any careful scrutiny of university research is apt to reveal weaknesses, it is more likely that these weaknesses will be quickly and systematically identified in the academic setting than elsewhere. Controversy is more likely to be resolved on grounds of scientific merit (i.e., by appeal to a relatively well-defined set of objective standards) than on grounds of political expediency or party loyalty.[8]

It would be presumptuous and no doubt unprofitable in the long run, however, to propose that all compensatory education programs be initiated in the academy. For one thing, there is some evidence that academicians are not notably successful in coping with the political factors that affect compensatory education programs (Moynihan 1969, chaps. 6, 7, and 8 passim).

---

[7] Examples are the Bereiter-Engelmann, Peabody Early Training, and Institute for Developmental Studies projects.

[8] On the other hand, it could be that programs which are created by academicians only seem more successful because they have good evaluative designs built into them, while programs not initiated by academicians which are highly innovative and successful are not known to be successful because their evaluative designs are poor.

In addition, the professor who becomes overinvolved in political processes outside the university runs an increasing risk of attack from within it, either from students or his colleagues. It would seem that a number of programs should continue to be locally based and funded and to be directed by persons long on ideas and experience if short on knowledge of how to justify their procedures.[9]

It must be recognized that relatively independent projects which encourage creative venturing are high-risk activities. The yield is apt to be quite low, and funds may appear wasted. However, they have the advantage of often developing a workable solution to a problem because the distracting and detailed specifications of the causes of the program's success are avoided. As Scriven (1967) has put it in a discussion of curriculum evaluation, "Even a course with gross over-simplifications, professionally repugnant though it may be to the academic expert, may be getting across a better idea of the truth about its subject than a highbrow competitor" (p. 58). The rationale and justification for these high-risk programs is that they can by-pass the time-consuming academic approach—including the built-in evaluation—and quickly arrive at a solution, which can then be examined to see why it works.

We have contrasted compensatory education programs which have careful evaluation built into them with high-risk, creative innovations which to some extent defy or preclude systematic evaluation. It would be useful to have a permanent interdisciplinary evaluation committee of behavioral scientists set up specifically to determine the relative success of

-----

[9]One partial remedy for this ignorance of methodology is proposed by Scriven (1967). He suggests giving such persons "an intensive short course in evaluation techniques and problems prior to their commencing work. Such a course would be topic-neutral, and would thereby avoid the problems of criticism of one's own 'baby.' Interaction with a professional evaluator can then be postponed substantially and should also be less anxiety-provoking" (p. 55).

programs[10] and to direct ongoing research. To some extent, organizations have sprung up in the private sector to do this: management consultant groups, whether competent or not, are tailoring their services to the needs of public agencies for this sort of evaluation.

To return to the dilemma mentioned above—the choice between sophisticated, carefully evaluated projects on which decisions can be based and high-risk projects which maximize the innovative abilities of their directors—we implied that the variable with which we are dealing is program specificity. This variable can be expressed reasonably well along a continuum:

	Minimum information from evaluation research	Maximum information from evaluation research	h i
l o w	Maximum possible creativity	Minimum possible creativity	g h

We would encourage three lines of action. First, as part of fund allocation and jurisdiction, a group of programs should be sponsored in which the method of evaluation is specified by committee. This would give the committee a group of control programs (a counterpart to control groups) which they could use to maximize the yield of statistical data of the type best suited to answer methodological questions. For example, if it were not known how long an Upward Bound subject should be

---

[10]It is noteworthy that an interagency staff group of HEW (March 4, 1969; Report to the Advisory Committee on Head-start) recommended the immediate creation of a committee representing federal agencies which have responsibilities related to early childhood development. The first priority for this committee would be to prepare, in collaboration with outside experts, a comprehensive plan for evaluation, research, and demonstration for the early childhood program. Such an interagency committee was formed for federal manpower research in 1967 to strengthen the research effort in the area and to aid in the dissemination and utilization of its results.

exposed to treatment or whether length of exposure makes any difference within certain boundaries, the evaluation committee might ask that programs be run for varying lengths of time to determine the effects of duration of exposure. Such a pool of control programs should be small, and the programs themselves should be viewed as part of the evaluation process. Perhaps the number of control programs would never be large enough to answer the researchers' multitude of substantive questions, but the attempt would be a step in the right direction, and scientific parsimony might result from administrative parsimony.

Our second recommendation is that a small number of programs be funded at the other end of the continuum, programs which would be purely speculative and high-risk; i.e., in addition to the possibility of low pay-off, they should proceed without excessive and slow evaluation.[11] The social urgency of compensatory education, we think, makes it in the public interest to find solutions quickly, which means funding novel, untried programs which do not have to be appraised immediately. The innovator must be given a chance to observe his idea in action and to make appropriate adjustments before a team of "statistics grabbers" emerges on the scene.

Third, the large majority of programs should fall into the category of compromise, in the middle of the continuum, where any evaluation has to make do with what is there. Of course, the primary objective is moving programs from the left to the right side of the continuum, where we can specify the conditions under which they will be successful.

Our recommendations are predicated on the belief that a more experimental approach to the problems experienced by social action programs is long overdue (Campbell 1969) and that adequate and reliable instruments will be developed to measure program success. Funds should be made available to

---

[11]It must be emphasized that absence of evaluation research does not in any sense mean absence of provisions for normal administrative review.

underwrite development of such instruments independent of any specific project. Unable to measure socioemotional change adequately, we are left with the propagandistic utterances of each project director as the basis for our policy decisions.

Our analysis of the existing evaluation research on compensatory education programs has led us to conclude that over all it fails to meet even minimum standards for program design, data collection, and data analysis. Over-all direction, rather than seemingly haphazard funding of any question which captures the interest of an investigator, is needed. We have suggested establishment of an interdisciplinary panel of social scientists and federal administrators to establish priorities and to specify the most feasible evaluation procedures to pursue in obtaining answers. Investigators should then be sought out to carry out the research desired. Because we are acutely aware of the price which is paid when one more level is added to the bureaucratic hierarchy in the familiar attempt to rationalize a given activity from beginning to end, we have opted for exempting a limited number of programs from the immediate scrutiny of such an evaluation team while placing a few others totally under its control.

Compensatory education programs now bear the burden of justifying their existence. No public school system in history has ever been abolished because it could not teach children to read and write, yet some compensatory programs, aimed at the very children who will probably be losers in the regular school program, could be in just this situation. They are being asked to succeed in less time than that allowed the regular school systems. Perhaps this is healthy: insistence on nothing less than success as a condition of survival can indeed provide great motivation. But those who condemn all compensatory programs out of hand should temper their criticism with the realization of the magnitude of the task confronted, the brief experience in coping with it, and the pitifully small fund of scientific knowledge relevant to the problems of disadvantaged children.

REFERENCES

American College Testing Program. 1968. Special Class Profile (1967 Upward Bound Bridge Class). Report to Educational Associates, Inc., Data Systems Office. Washington, D.C.

Atkinson, R. C. 1968. Computer-Based Instruction in Initial Reading. In Proceedings of the 1967 Invitational Conference on Testing Problems. Princeton, N.J.: Educational Testing Service.

Atkinson, R. C., and Wilson, H. A. 1968. Computer-Assisted Instruction. Science 162:73–77.

Bereiter, C. 1967. Instructional Planning in Early Compensatory Education. Phi Delta Kappan 48:355–59.

Bereiter, C., and Engelmann, S. 1966. Teaching Disadvantaged Children in the Preschool. Englewood Cliffs, N.J.: Prentice-Hall.

Bloom, B. S. 1964. Stability and Change in Human Characteristics. New York: John Wiley & Sons.

_____. 1966. Stability and Change in Human Characteristics: Implications for School Reorganization. Educational Administration Quarterly 2:35–49.

Brickner, C. A. 1969. An Experimental Program Designed to Increase Auditory Discrimination with Headstart Children. Paper presented at A.E.R.A. meeting, Los Angeles, California.

Bruner, J. S. 1961. The Process of Education. Cambridge, Mass.: Harvard University Press.

_____. 1966. Toward a Theory of Instruction. New York: W. W. Norton.

Campbell, D. T. 1957. Factors Relevant to the Validity of Experiments in Social Settings. Psychological Bulletin 54:297–312.

_____. 1969. Reforms as Experiments. American Psychologist 24:409–29.

Chorost, S. B., et al. 1967. An Evaluation of the Effects of a Summer Head Start Program. ERIC document no. ED 014 327.

Coleman, J. S., et al. 1966. Equality of Educational Opportunity. Washington, D.C.: U.S. Government Printing Office.

Cronbach, L. J. 1969. Heredity, Environment, and Educational Policy. Harvard Educational Review 39:338–47.

Dentler, R. A. February, 1969. Urban Eyewash: A Review of "Title I/Year II." The Urban Review, pp. 32–33.

Deutsch, M. 1967. The Disadvantaged Child. New York: Basic Books.

_____. November, 1968. Research and Evaluation, Part II. New York: Institute for Developmental Studies, New York University.

Educational Associates, Inc. 1967–68. Idea Exchange. Monthly publication reporting on Upward Bound to the U.S. Office of Economic Opportunity.

_____. December, 1968. Upward Bound, Semi-Annual Report to the Office of Economic Opportunity. Washington, D.C.

Elkind, D. 1969. Piagetian and Psychometric Conceptions of Intelligence. Harvard Educational Review 39:319–37.

Froomkin, J. 1968. Students and Buildings. U.S. Office of Education report OE-50054.

Gardenhire, J. F. September, 1968. Study of College Retention of 1965 & 1966 UPWARD BOUND Bridge Students. Report to the U.S. Office of Economic Opportunity by Educational Associates, Inc. Washington, D.C.

Gordon, E. W., and Jablonsky, A. 1967. Compensatory Education in the Equalization of Educational Opportunity. In National Conference on Equal Educational Opportunity in America's Cities. Washington, D.C.: U.S. Commission on Civil Rights.

Gordon, E. W., and Wilkerson, D. 1966. Compensatory Education for the Disadvantaged. New York: College Entrance Examination Board.

74

Granger, R. L., et al. June, 1969. The Impact of Head Start. An Evaluation of the Effects of Head Start on Children's Cognitive and Affective Development. Vol. 1. Report to the U.S. Office of Economic Opportunity by Westinghouse Learning Corporation and Ohio University.

Greenleigh Associates, Inc. January, 1969. Upward Bound: A Study of Impact on the Secondary School and the Community. Report to the U.S. Office of Economic Opportunity.

Guilford, J. P. 1954. Psychometric Methods. New York: McGraw-Hill.

Hawkridge, D. G.; Chalupsky, A. B.; and Roberts, A. O. H. 1968. A Study of Selected Exemplary Programs for the Education of Disadvantaged Children. U.S. Office of Education final report, project 089013.

Hawkridge, D. G.; Tallmadge, G. K.; and Larsen, J. K. 1968. Foundations for Success in Educating Disadvantaged Children. U.S. Office of Education final report, project 107143.

Headstart Childhood Research Information Bulletin. 1969. Vol. 1. Washington, D.C.: National Laboratory on Early Childhood Education, ERIC Center.

Hodges, W. L., and Spicker, H. H. 1967. The Effects of Pre-school Experiences on Culturally Deprived Children. Young Children 23:23–43.

Howe, H., II. 1967. National Ideals and Educational Policy. In National Conference on Equal Educational Opportunity in America's Cities. Washington, D.C.: U.S. Commission on Civil Rights.

Hunt, D. E., and Hardt, R. H. Characterization of UPWARD BOUND Summer 1966; Characterization of UPWARD BOUND Academic Year 1967; Characterization of UP-WARD BOUND 1967–1968. Syracuse, N.Y.: Syracuse University Youth Development Center.

Hunt, J. McV. 1969a. Black Genes—White Environment. Trans-Action 6:12–22.

——. 1969b. Has Compensatory Education Failed? Has It Been Attempted? Harvard Educational Review 39:278–300.

Improving the Opportunities and Achievements of the Children of the Poor. February, 1965. Report to the U.S. Office of Economic Opportunity by a panel of authorities on child development.

Jaeger, R. M. 1969. The 1968 Survey on Compensatory Education. Paper presented at A.E.R.A. meeting, Los Angeles, California.

Jensen, A. R. 1969. How Much Can We Boost IQ and Scholastic Achievement? Harvard Educational Review 39:1–123.

Kagan, J. S. 1969. Inadequate Evidence and Illogical Conclusions. Harvard Educational Review 39:274–77.

Karnes, M. B. 1968. A Research Program to Determine the Effects of Various Preschool Intervention Programs on the Development of Disadvantaged Children and the Strategic Age for Such Intervention. Paper presented at A.E.R.A. meeting, Chicago, Illinois.

Klaus, R. A., and Gray, S. W. 1968. The Early Training Project for Disadvantaged Children: A Report after Five Years. Monographs of the Society for Research in Child Development, Inc., vol. 33, no. 4. Chicago: University of Chicago Press.

Kornegay, F. A. 1968a. College Enrollment of Former Upward Bound Students: A Profile and Summary. Idea Exchange, 3, no. 11, pp. 24–26.

——. 1968b. Sample Study of 1967 Bridge Students into Spring Semester 1968. Report to the U.S. Office of Economic Opportunity by Educational Associates, Inc. Washington, D.C.

Krist, M. W. 1967. What Types of Compensatory Education Programs Are Effective? In National Conference on Equal Educational Opportunity in America's Cities. Washington, D.C.: U.S. Commission on Civil Rights.

McDavid, J. W., et al. N.d. Project Headstart Evaluation and Research Summary, 1965–1967. Washington, D.C.: U.S. Office of Economic Opportunity, Project Headstart, Division of Research and Evaluation.

McDill, E. L., Rigsby, L. C., and Meyers, E. D., Jr. 1969. Educational Climates of High Schools: Their Effects and Sources. The American Journal of Sociology 74:567–86.

Miller, H. L., ed. 1969. Education for the Disadvantaged. New York: Free Press of Glencoe.

Moynihan, D. P. 1969. Maximum Feasible Misunderstanding. New York: Free Press of Glencoe.

New Republic. 1969. How Head a Head Start? April 26, 1969, pp. 8–9.

New York Times. 1969a. Dispute over Value of Head Start. April 20, 1969, p. 11E.

_____. 1969b. Finch Criticizes Head Start Study. April 25, 1969, p. 22.

Nichols, R. C. 1968. Review of U.S. Commission on Civil Rights, Racial Isolation in the Public Schools. American Educational Research Journal 5:700–707.

Nixon, R. M. February 19, 1969. Economic Opportunity Act. Message to the Congress of the United States released by the White House Press Secretary.

Piaget, J. 1952. The Origins of Intelligence in Children. New York: International Universities Press.

_____. 1963. The Psychology of Intelligence. Englewood Cliffs, N.J.: Prentice-Hall.

Pines, M. 1967. Revolution in Learning: The Years from Birth to Six. New York: Harper and Row.

Posner, J. April, 1968. Evaluation of "Successful" Projects in Compensatory Education. U.S. Office of Education, Office of Planning and Evaluation, occasional paper no. 8.

Rossi, P. H. 1969. Practice, Method, and Theory in Evaluating Social Action Programs. In On Fighting Poverty, ed. J. L. Sundquist. New York: Basic Books.

Rusk, B. A. 1969. An Evaluation of a Six-Week Headstart Program Using an Academically Oriented Curriculum: Canton, 1967. Paper presented at A.E.R.A. meeting, Los Angeles, California.

Scriven, M. 1967. The Methodology of Evaluation. In Perspectives of Curriculum Evaluation, ed. R. W. Tyler, R. M. Gagné, and M. Scriven. Chicago: Rand McNally and Co.

Shea, P. August, 1967. Upward Bound Early Progress, Problems and Promise in Educational Escape from Poverty. Report to the U.S. Office of Economic Opportunity.

Suppes, P. September, 1966. The Uses of Computers in Education. Scientific American, pp. 207–20.

Suppes, P., and Morningstar, M. 1969. Evaluation of Three Computer-Assisted Instruction Programs. Stanford University Institute for Mathematical Studies in the Social Sciences technical report 142. Stanford, Calif.: Stanford University.

U.S. Commission on Civil Rights. 1967. Racial Isolation in the Public Schools. Vol. 1. Washington, D.C.: U.S. Government Printing Office.

U.S. Department of Health, Education, and Welfare, Office of Education. 1966. The First Year of Title I, ESEA: The States Report. Washington, D.C.: U.S. Government Printing Office.

_____. March 7, 1969. Headstart Report. Report to the Advisory Committee on Headstart.

_____. March 4, 1969. Report to the Advisory Committee on Headstart.

_____. N.d. Title I/Year II. The Second Annual Report of Title I of the Elementary and Secondary Education Act of 1965, School Year 1966–1967. Washington, D.C.: U.S. Government Printing Office.

U.S. Office of Economic Opportunity, Project Headstart, Division of Research and Evaluation. January, 1968. Research and Evaluation, Project Headstart. Washington, D.C.: Office of Economic Opportunity.

_____. 1968. Upward Bound Policy Guidelines 1969–1970. Office of Economic Opportunity Handbook 6118–1. Washington, D.C.: Office of Economic Opportunity.

Weinberg, M. 1968. Desegregation Research: An Appraisal. Bloomington, Ind.: Phi Delta Kappan.

Wrightstone, J. W., et al. 1965. Evaluation of the Higher Horizons Program for Underprivileged Children, a Summary. U.S. Office of Education, Cooperative Research Project no. 1124.

Zimiles, H. 1969. Review of M. Deutsch, The Disadvantaged Child. Harvard Educational Review 39:177–80.

INDEX

Academic Preschool Program.
See Bereiter-Engelmann Academic Preschool Program
Action research: problems in, 5; role of policy-maker in, 6; social scientist and, 6
American College Testing Program, 34
Aptitudes of students: and school achievement, 62
Attitudes of students: and school achievement, 62

Banneker project, 36–38
Bereiter, C., 11, 56
Bereiter-Engelmann Academic Preschool Program, 3n, 36, 39, 58–61, 67n: parental involvement in, 59; pupil-teacher ratio in, 59; teacher training in, 59–60
"Black box" strategy, 9, 47
Bloom, B. S., 7, 10
Bruner, J. S., 8

California Achievement Tests, 40
Campbell, D. T., 7n, 27, 70
Center for Urban Education, 30n
Chalupsky, A. B., 9, 42n, 45, 55, 59
"Charismatic innovator": in demonstration projects, 50–51
Chorost, S. B., 52n
Civil Rights Commission, U.S., 55
Coleman, J. S., 10n, 12, 58n
Compensatory education: alleged failure of, 1; definition of, 1; reasons for failure of, 2–4; relation to school desegregation, 55n; strategies for successful, 55–71; successful and unsuccessful programs, 58–65; vagueness of objectives, 46. See also Local compensatory programs

Computer Assisted Instruction, 41, 49
Concept formation: and Peabody project, 62
Concept Inventory test, 11
Control groups, 53–54: contamination of, 54, 61; distal, 65; within intact groups, 54
"Control of environment": and academic achievement, 12
Crisis Teachers program, 50
Cronbach, L., 1
"Cultural enrichment": ambiguity of, as program goal, 47

Delay of gratification: and school achievement, 62
"Delayed effects": and program evaluation, 9
Dentler, R. A., 29–30
Deutsch, M., 7, 41n, 48
Development, intellectual: process of, 7–13
Diagnostically Based Curriculum for Pre-School Deprived Children, 41

Early Training Project (Peabody College), 37, 39, 49, 54, 61–65, 67n
Educational Associates Inc., 34n, 35
Elkind, D., 3
Engelmann, S., 11. See also Bereiter-Engelmann Academic Preschool Program
Evaluation, program: "formative," 49; immediate, pressures for, 45; interdisciplinary committee for, 68–69, 71; "intrinsic," 47; "pay-off," 47; strategies for, 66–71; "summative," 49

"Fadeout effect," 18, 40, 51–52: and Bereiter-Engelmann program, 59–60; and Early Training

DISCHARGED

MAY 17
DISCHARGED

DISCHARGED 1973

DISCHARGED

DISCHARGED

DISCHARGED

DISCHARGED 1873

DISCHARGED 73

MAY
DISCHARGED

DISCHARGED

DISCHARGED

DISCHARGED 1980